Short Bike Rides®
on Long Island

Short Bike Rides® Series

Short Bike Rides®
on Long Island

Fifth Edition

By
Phil Angelillo

The Globe Pequot Press

Guilford, Connecticut

Cover photo: Chris Dubé
Cover design: Saralyn D'Amato

Library of Congress Cataloging-in-Publication Data
Angelillo, Phil.
    Short bike rides on Long Island / by Phil Angelillo. — 5th ed.
        p.   cm. — (Short bike rides series)
    ISBN 0-7627-0208-7
    1. Bicycle touring—New York (State)—Long Island—Guidebooks.
    2. Long Island (N.Y.)—Guidebooks. I. Title. II. Series.
GV1045.5.N72L663   1998
917.47'210443—dc21   97-44041
                                                                 CIP

♻ This book is printed on recycled paper.
Manufactured in the United States of America
Fifth Edition/Sixth Printing

Help Us Keep This Guide Up to Date

Every effort has been made by the author and editors to make this guide as accurate and useful as possible. However, many things can change after a guide is published–establishments close, phone numbers change, hiking trails are rerouted, facilities come under new management, etc.

We would love to hear from you concerning your experiences with this guide and how you feel it could be made better and be kept up to date. While we may not be able to respond to all comments and suggestions, we'll take them to heart and we'll also make certain to share them with the author. Please send your comments and suggestions to the following address:

The Globe Pequot Press
Reader Response/Editorial Department
P.O. Box 480
Guilford, CT 06437

Or you may e-mail us at:

editorial@globe-pequot.com

Thanks for your input, and happy travels!

Contents

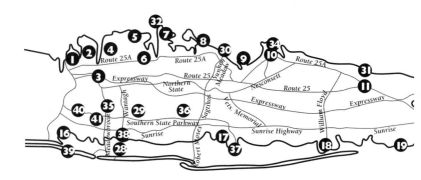

Off-shore Rides

Bike Paths, Park Paths, Boardwalks and Bikeways

Introduction

Long Island is a cyclist's delight. Its contrasting environments, long history, and varied social makeup provide a kaleidoscope of attractions and scenery, all of it on generally easy bicycling terrain. This book presents a variety of rides that explore the areas of Long Island that best display its essential character and unique historical and geographic features. They span the island from the New York City border to the easternmost tips of its flukes and beyond, along flat Atlantic Ocean seashore, wooded hills on the Long Island Sound shore, bountiful farms, picturesque villages steeped in colonial history, and bustling modern new towns.

The rides vary in length from 8 to 30 miles and are laid out for a leisurely half day or so of bicycling with ample opportunities for resting at points of scenic or historical interest. In addition, detailed descriptions of bike paths in Long Island's extensive park system are provided that present the best facilities for a good bike ride in a traffic-free environment. Each ride description includes a map, detailed road instructions, and information on the ride's length, duration, terrain, and traffic conditions. These are accompanied by a general description of the ride area, its points of interest, and, where necessary, the bicycling difficulties that can be expected along the way.

An Overview

Ralph Henry Gabriel, in his excellent little book, *The Evolution of Long Island,* suggests that the character of the island stems from the interplay of the physical force of the surrounding sea and the social force of people and ideas issuing from New York City. The rides in this book explore the most interesting results of this mingling to provide the cyclist with a mosaic of experiences of what Long Island is and was.

Geologically, the island is known for its long, wide, white sand beaches on the Atlantic, its craggy inlets and harbors on Long Island Sound, and the flat terrain between—the result of glacial actions eons ago. The remains of the activity are visible on several of the rides: at Wading River and other points along the Sound shore where the bluffs carved from glacial debris stand silently facing the Sound; and in the convoluted peninsulas and harbors seen on the western north shore rides. The outwash beaches of the south shore of the Atlantic, Long Island's premier summer attraction, are toured in the Montauk and Hampton rides of the east end, farther west at Smith Point, and at Long Beach near the New York City border. Soils formed from glacial deposits were later developed into rich farmlands such as those seen on the rides through Wading River, Riverhead, Mattituck, Southold, and Orient Point on the island's north fork and Bridgehampton on the south fork.

Farming and fishing supported the island's early settlers, and a good deal remains of the colonial past on the ride routes through the island's eastern parts at Southold, Southampton, and Sag Harbor and north shore at Stony Brook, Port Jefferson, Smithtown, Huntington, and Northport. Other ride routes go through areas whose attractions date from more recent times, tracing the advance of urban development from New York City eastward on former farmland and scrub. Thus we get the estates seen on the rides through Great Neck, Manhasset, Glen Cove, and Oyster Bay on the north shore, and on the south shore, the closely packed communities of the Five Towns and Long Beach. The still-continuing expansion is evident farther east in the rides through Great River and Smith Point. Two special rides, Shelter Island and Block Island, provide replicas in miniature of the total Long Island topography of sea views, beaches, farms, and villages.

The evolution of Long Island continues, of course, and the underlying causes of change remain. No doubt these ride routes in the future will traverse communities vastly different from those that exist today—but they will probably be just as interesting for the cyclist to explore.

About the Rides

To the greatest extent possible, the ride material is presented to ease map and road direction reading when under way. Accordingly, the maps are located directly opposite the ride directions, and in most cases the directions are presented on a single page. Further, the directions are segmented to allow point-to-point riding. In almost all cases, these points on the road are clearly visible road signs, although in a few places unique landmarks or other features are used. It is suggested that the description of the ride be read in its entirety before riding to know beforehand the points of interest along the way (also noted on the maps), doing away with the need to refer to this material while pedaling.

The mileages in the ride directions are approximate distances. In most of the rides alternate, shorter routes are also provided. The time indicated is approximate pedaling time while cycling at a sightseeing pace. It does not include extended rests at points of interest. Hilly terrain implies a ride in which the casual weekend cyclist will encounter some hills that will probably have to be walked; moderately hilly has less strenuous hills; rides designated as flat should be no problem at all. All the rides have been laid out to minimize riding in traffic, but even so, most rides have one or more segments in which some traffic will be encountered. The directions give a realistic assessment of what can be expected.

The path and boardwalk rides capitalize on Long Island's unmatched park facilities. In most of them, bicycling can be augmented with other activities such as swimming or picnicking that make the ride ideal for a full-day family outing. Because they are free of automobile traffic, the paths are a must for those just learning to ride or sharpening skills fashioned in the past and for groups with children.

A Note on Safety

Traffic is heaviest in Nassau and western Suffolk but must be anticipated in all areas. The requirements for safe riding are simple enough—a bicycle in good working condition, defensive and alert riding, and a measure of common sense. The roads are there for autos and bicycles alike, and the cyclist is responsible no less than the motorist for full knowledge of, and conformance with, the rules of the road.

Cyclists should:
- Ride on the right in the direction of traffic.
- Use hand signals when turning.
- Obey traffic signals and stop signs.
- When riding in a group, keep to the right in single file, keeping an adequate distance between riders.
- Make sure each bicycle has reliable brakes, a bell or horn for warning, and a headlight and rear and side reflectors for night riding.
- Wear a protective helmet and bright clothing.

In addition, everyone should be prepared for common bicycling hazards such as sandy patches on curves, potholes and sewer gratings, railroad-track crossings, and in urban areas, the sudden opening of parked car doors. Keep in mind that traffic is lightest on Sunday mornings, making the rides most enjoyable during these hours.

Although the roads should be shared equally, the realities of bicycling suggest that the rider not argue too strongly with motorized traffic for the right-of-way—it makes sense to yield. Finally, if you are at all unsure of your capability at bicycling, it is advisable to practice on the described traffic-free bike and park paths before attempting street riding.

• • •

While these rides by no means exhaust the interesting bicycling routes that could be explored on Long Island, they would probably rank high on most cyclists' lists of the best the island has to offer.

Great Neck

Number of miles:	13
Approximate pedaling time:	2 hours
Terrain:	Moderately hilly
Surface:	Good
Traffic:	Heavy in town, moderate elsewhere
Things to see:	Saddle Rock Grist Mill, Stepping Stone Park, U.S. Merchant Marine Academy

This is a pleasant ride around the Great Neck peninsula, an area very much in demand by people who wish to remain within easy traveling distance of New York City while living in gracious suburban surroundings. There are outstanding water views all along its coasts on Little Neck Bay, Manhassett Bay, and Long Island Sound. From its northwest shore one can even see New York's skyscrapers and bridges. There are not many areas that can match Great Neck in convenience and charm, a fact that is reflected in the price of real estate and housing hereabouts.

The ride begins in the Shoreward parking lot south of the railroad station in the village of Great Neck Plaza. Parking is available to all on Sundays but is limited to Great Neck residents on weekdays and Saturdays. There are other parking lots, however, in shopping centers along Great Neck Road west of Middle Neck Road. Great Neck Plaza is the shopping and commuting center of the peninsula, and so it can be quite crowded and heavily trafficked. Once out of this immediate area, however, things quiet down.

From Great Neck Plaza the ride goes north on Bayview Avenue to the Saddle Rock Grist Mill. This is one of the most popular historical attractions on Long Island because it maintains the feel of handmade

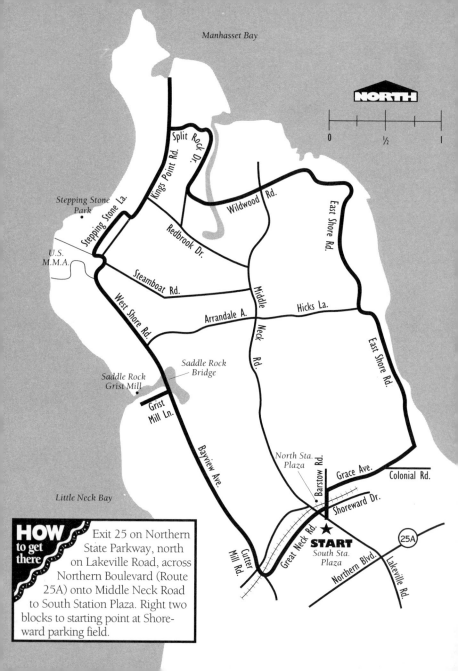

- Start at the Shoreward parking field two blocks east of Middle Neck Road, south of the railroad tracks on Shoreward Drive.
- Out of the Shoreward parking lot, right on Shoreward Drive, across Middle Neck Road onto Great Neck Road, to Cutter Mill Road.
- Right at Cutter Mill Road, which immediately merges with Bayview Avenue on the left, for about 1¾ miles on Bayview, to Grist Mill Lane on the left. Signs indicate the approach to the grist mill.
- Left on Grist Mill Lane to the Saddle Rock Grist Mill.
- Return to Bayview Avenue (which becomes West Shore Road farther on), and go left over Saddle Rock Bridge for 1¼ miles to Kings Point Road.
- Right on Kings Point Road to Steamboat Road.
- Left on Steamboat Road to the Merchant Marine Academy.
- From the academy go left on Stepping Stone Lane, adjacent to Stepping Stone Park on the left, around to Kings Point Road.
- Left on Kings Point Road for about 1½ miles to its end.
- Return on Kings Point Road for about ¾ mile to Split Rock Drive on the left.
- Left on Split Rock Drive to Wildwood Road.
- Left on Wildwood Road, circling across Middle Neck Road onto East Shore Road.
- Continue on East Shore Road for 3¼ miles along Manhasset Bay to Grace Avenue. About halfway along this leg, East Shore Road turns left at the junction with Hicks Lane.
- Right on Grace Avenue past the Colonial Road merge for about 1 mile to Barstow Road.
- Left on Barstow Road across North Station Plaza to Shoreward Drive on the left.
- Left on Shoreward Drive to the Shoreward parking lot and the ride starting point.

colonial buildings and the workaday world of the past. Corn is ground at the mill for demonstration purposes, and the various processes of milling, historic and current, are described in attractive displays.

The ride proceeds north from the grist mill over the Saddle Rock Bridge to Steamboat Road and the U.S. Merchant Marine Academy. The Academy's sixty-eight acres and several buildings are worth seeing, especially the former Walter Chrysler estate on Long Island Sound, now part of the academy grounds. In the spring and fall, regimental reviews can be viewed on Saturday mornings.

Immediately north of the academy is Stepping Stone Park. There is no better view of Long Island Sound from Great Neck than from this park. On summer Sundays, the Sound is alive with sailboats. The park abounds with Frisbee players, toddlers, and *New York Times* readers, producing so pleasant a stop that many cyclists won't bother to go any farther.

Those who do, however, can continue north on Kings Point Road to Kings Point. The road dead-ends at a very peaceful and tranquil community of attractive homes on an inlet of Long Island Sound. Proceeding south from here the ride continues through wooded Kings Point to the east shore of the peninsula on Manhasset Bay. On East Shore Road for half its length is a wetlands strip containing a variety of marsh vegetation and wildlife.

On reentering the village of Great Neck, the surroundings become more commercial. Grace Avenue, the last leg of the ride, is a challenging uphill climb that may have to be walked. There are plenty of places near Shoreward parking field, however, to get cool refreshments, and you might also enjoy a stroll through the hubbub of Great Neck's shopping area along Middle Neck Road.

Manhasset—Port Washington

Number of miles:	17 (short ride 11)
Approximate pedaling time:	3½ hours (short ride 2 hours)
Terrain:	Moderately hilly
Surface:	Good
Traffic:	Heavy in towns, moderate elsewhere
Things to see:	North Hempstead Town Dock, Sands Point Preserve, Hempstead Harbor Park

This ride takes you through some of the finest residential areas on Long Island. The Port Washington peninsula, or Manhasset Neck, is the site of a number of communities of impressive homes and estates, some dating from the nineteenth century. This peninsula, with Great Neck to the west and Oyster Bay to the east, makes up the "Gold Coast" of Long Island, signifying a sumptuous lifestyle made famous by F. Scott Fitzgerald. A good deal of "Great Gatsby" ambience remains, especially in the Sands Point area at the northern end of the peninsula.

The ride starts at Manhasset Green Park in the village of Manhasset and proceeds north on Plandome Road past Leeds Pond Preserve and the North Shore Science Museum in Plandome Manor. Plandome Road is narrow and shoulderless in this area and should be cycled with care. The causeway leading to the entrance of the preserve affords the first unobstructed view of Manhasset Bay. The preserve and museum offer guided walks through typical local wildlife habitats. Bicycling within the preserve is not allowed, however.

Continuing north we arrive at the North Hempstead Town Dock at Port Washington. There are several excellent restaurants here, although the meals they offer are more suitable for dinner than for cy-

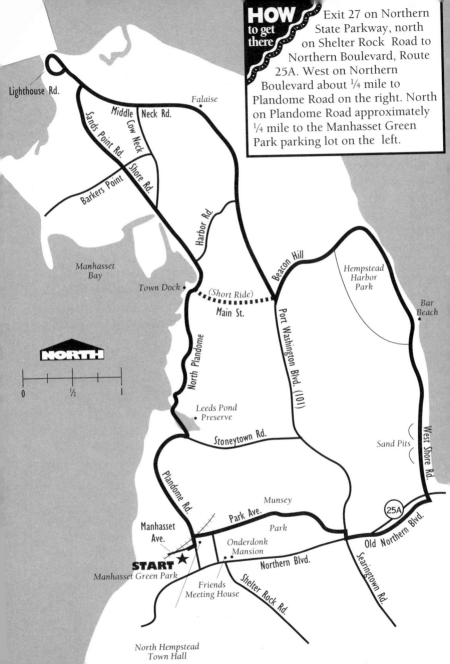

HOW to get there

Exit 27 on Northern State Parkway, north on Shelter Rock Road to Northern Boulevard, Route 25A. West on Northern Boulevard about ¼ mile to Plandome Road on the right. North on Plandome Road approximately ¼ mile to the Manhasset Green Park parking lot on the left.

Lighthouse Rd.

Middle Neck Rd.

Cow Neck

Sands Point Rd.

Shore Rd.

Barkers Point

Falaise

Harbor Rd.

Beacon Hill

Hempstead Harbor Park

Manhasset Bay

Town Dock

(Short Ride)

Main St.

Port Washington Blvd. (101)

Bar Beach

NORTH

0   ½   1

North Plandome

Leeds Pond Preserve

Stoneytown Rd.

Sand Pits

West Shore Rd.

Plandome Rd.

Park Ave.

Munsey

Park

Manhasset Ave.

Onderdonk Mansion

25A

Old Northern Blvd.

START

Manhasset Green Park

Friends Meeting House

Northern Blvd.

Shelter Rock Rd.

Searingtown Rd.

North Hempstead Town Hall

- Start from Manhasset Green Park on Plandome Road and Manhasset Avenue, just south of the Manhasset railroad station.
- Out to Plandome Road and left approximately 1½ miles to Leeds Pond Preserve.
- From the preserve, continue right for about 1¼ miles on Plandome Road past the town dock to Shore Road on the left, at the beginning of the uphill section of Main Street in Port Washington.
- For the short ride, continue on Main Street for about 1 mile to Port Washington Boulevard. Go left on Port Washington Boulevard one block to Beacon Hill Road on the right. Go right on Beacon Hill Road to West Shore Road.
- For the full ride, continue left on Shore Road (which becomes Sands Point Road) for about 2¾ miles to Middle Neck Road.
- Go left on Middle Neck Road to its end, with Lighthouse Road on the left.
- Go left on Lighthouse Road around back to Middle Neck Road.
- Right on Middle Neck Road approximately 1½ miles to Sands Point Preserve (Falaise) on the left, then 2½ miles to Beacon Hill Road on the left in Port Washington.
- Go left on Beacon Hill Road 1 mile to West Shore Road.
- Continue on West Shore Road, bordering Hempstead Harbor, to Hempstead Harbor Park and Bar Beach, then on for about 3 miles to Old Northern Boulevard on the right, indicated by a "Truck Route" sign immediately past the Northern Boulevard overpass and Mott Avenue.
- Go right on Old Northern Boulevard to the merge with Northern Boulevard, Route 25A, then continue west on 25A about ¼ mile to Port Washington Boulevard—Route 101.
- Go right on Port Washington Boulevard one block to Park Avenue in Munsey Park on the left.
- Go left on Park Avenue for about 2 miles to Plandome Road in Manhasset. Friends Meeting House and Onderdonk Mansion are

on Northern Boulevard five blocks south of Park Avenue at Onderdonk Avenue.

- Go left on Plandome Road back to the ride starting point at Manhasset Green Park.

---

clists' light lunches. The dock itself runs out into Manhasset Bay and is a nice place to stop for a cold drink and a view of the bay with private boats running in and out.

We continue on Main Street from the town dock up a steep hill to Shore Road, which intersects from the left. Those wishing to take the short ride should continue straight ahead on Main Street through Port Washington to Port Washington Boulevard, picking up the route again at Beacon Hill Road. The full ride continues north to Sands Point. An immediate change is evident on entering Sands Point, as the surroundings become almost rural. In this area is a mix of fine old homes and large new ones located on spacious and attractive grounds. At the end of Middle Neck Road we come to the very end of the peninsula at Sands Point. Lighthouse Road provides a striking water view and setting for the modernistic homes along it.

Proceeding south from Sands Point we come to the Sands Point Preserve, the site of Falaise, a large estate featuring a palatial French Norman-style manor house built in 1923 for Henry F. Guggenheim. Reservations must be made in advance to see the mansion, but it is worth it if you are interested in examining the living conditions of the very wealthy—twenty-six rooms, Spanish and French furnishings, sculpture, paintings, sailing trophies, and so on.

South from Falaise we come to Beacon Hill Road in Port Washington. This is a steep climb to the east side of the peninsula and may require some walking. From the top of the hill, West Shore Road sweeps down and around the edge of Hempstead Bay, offering a panoramic view along the way. Hempstead Harbor Park and Bar Beach are pleasant stops for resting after the Beacon Hill climb. To the right of West Shore Road, south of Bar Beach, is a grim example of what years of sand mining can do to such a scenic area. Notice the houses perched just back from the rim of the pit.

The last part of the ride goes along West Shore Road to the base of the peninsula and then heads west, back to Manhasset. Expect heavy traffic on the short segment on Northern Boulevard and Port Washington Boulevard into Munsey Park. Munsey Park, near Onderdonk Avenue and Northern Boulevard, is a pleasant, well-tended suburban community with lots of clipped grass and new homes. Toward the end of the Park Avenue leg is the Friends Meeting House and, next to it, the Onderdonk Mansion. The former, built in 1812, has the expected spare lean look and is in marked contrast to the columned robustness of the latter, built for Henry Gates Onderdonk in 1836.

Roslyn—Old Westbury

Number of miles:	8
Approximate pedaling time:	1½ hours
Terrain:	Moderately hilly
Surface:	Good
Traffic:	Moderate to heavy
Things to see:	Robeson-Williams Gristmill, Roslyn Clock Tower, Roslyn Historic District, Old Westbury Gardens

The town of Roslyn is nestled at the head of Hempstead Harbor, almost hidden from view from the autos whizzing by it on Route 25A on the elevated Roslyn Viaduct. It is a delightful place, however, to savor a vestige of Long Island's past. Within a half mile or so of the village is one of the most extensive communities of colonial and nineteenth-century homes and buildings that can be found on Long Island. For cyclists, it is an excellent starting point and terminus for an interesting ride through the estate country of Old Westbury and attractive modern suburban communities.

The ride starts from any of the parking lots on Old Northern Boulevard in Roslyn. The village dates from colonial times when the stream flowing into Hempstead Harbor was harnessed for milling. As happened on this and many other streams, the mill formed the nucleus of commercial activity for the surrounding agricultural lands leading to the development of the town.

On Old Northern Boulevard stands the Robeson-Williams Gristmill. The mill was built around 1700 and has since been restored. To the west, toward Main Street, is Washington Manor on Northern Boulevard. The building dates from 1758 and is now a restaurant. Guess who slept here in the summer of 1790? Across the

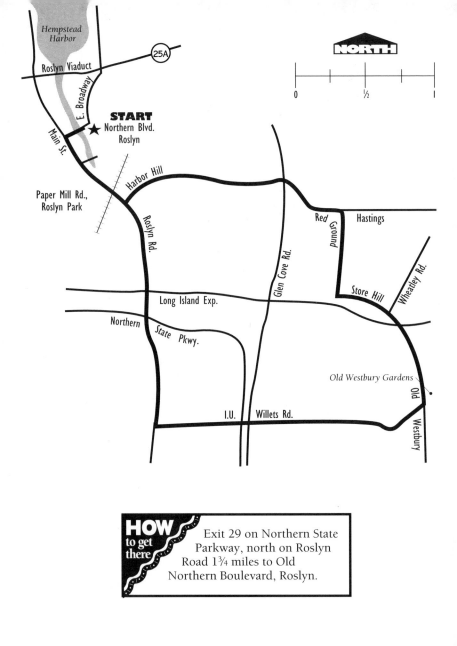

Hempstead
Harbor

25A

NORTH

0 ½ 1

Roslyn Viaduct

E. Broadway

START
★ Northern Blvd.
Roslyn

Main St.

Harbor Hill

Paper Mill Rd.,
Roslyn Park

Roslyn Rd.

Red Ground

Hastings

Glen Cove Rd.

Wheatley Rd.

Store Hill

Long Island Exp.

Northern State Pkwy.

Old Westbury Gardens

Old Westbury

I.U.   Willets Rd.

HOW
to get
there

Exit 29 on Northern State
Parkway, north on Roslyn
Road 1¾ miles to Old
Northern Boulevard, Roslyn.

DIREC-TIONS at a glance

- Start at one of the parking lots on Old Northern Boulevard in Roslyn.
- West from the parking lot to Main Street.
- Left on Main Street, which becomes Roslyn Road, through the Roslyn Historic District.
- Continue on Roslyn Road for about 2¾ miles, passing under the Long Island Railroad tracks and Long Island Expressway, and then over Northern State Parkway, to I. U. Willets Road.
- Left on I. U. Willets Road for approximately 2 miles, over Northern State Parkway to its end at Old Westbury Road.
- Left on Old Westbury Road to Old Westbury Gardens on the right.
- From Old Westbury Gardens, continue right on Old Westbury Road for about ¾ mile, over the Long Island Expressway to Store Hill Road, the expressway (westbound) service road.
- Left on Store Hill Road, past Wheatley Road, for about ½ mile to Red Ground Road.
- Right on Red Ground Road for about 1¼ miles to the intersection with Glen Cove Road and Harbor Hill Road. (Red Ground Road goes left at the junction with Hastings Road, halfway along this leg.)
- Straight across the intersection onto Harbor Hill Road; then on for about 1½ miles back to Roslyn Road.
- Right on Roslyn Road to Roslyn Park on the right.
- Continue through the park and Paper Mill Road back to ride starting point.

way is the Roslyn Clock Tower, built in 1895, and farther along on Main Street, Roslyn's Historic District. On Main Street between Old Northern Boulevard and East Broadway, stand about forty homes built between 1690 and 1865. Some are in excellent condition, and several are being restored.

The ride continues on Main Street onto Roslyn Road, passing under the Long Island Railroad on an uphill climb, usually with heavy traffic, past Roslyn High School, to Roslyn Heights. After passing the Long Island Expressway and Northern State Parkway, we enter Albertson. Here we find a typical higher-priced, but somewhat bland, modern suburban community on flat terrain.

After turning left at I. U. Willets Road, the ride progresses into Old Westbury at Glen Cove Road, and an immediate change in landscape is noticed. There are fewer homes, more and larger trees, and in some spots, full forest growth.

Turning left on Old Westbury Road we come immediately to the Old Westbury Gardens and Mansion. This is the former estate of the Phipps family, containing a huge eighteenth-century Georgian-style manor house built in 1906 and acres of manicured lawns shaded by tall, graceful trees. The estate also contains a formal Italian garden and an arboretum. It's a good place to stop and rest and experience for a while the good life of the very wealthy.

From Old Westbury Gardens we continue on Old Westbury Road over the Long Island Expressway onto the expressway's westbound service road. This is a bleak, open stretch that is best crossed quickly to regain good cycling country at Red Ground Road. Along Red Ground Road are fine large homes and heavily treed estates. At its end is a wide intersection at which Red Ground, Glen Cove, and Harbor Hill roads meet. Go directly across onto Harbor Hill Road, which continues down to Roslyn Road where we turn right, back toward Roslyn.

We enter the Roslyn Historic District at Main Street. Down a short way is Paper Mill Road and Roslyn Park on the right. On Paper Mill Road is Valentine House, built around 1800 and rebuilt around 1865. It now houses the Roslyn Village Hall. Farther on in Roslyn Park is a replica of the Onderdonk Paper Mill, New York's first paper mill, built around 1770. From here we continue back to Northern Boulevard and the starting point of the ride. You might be ready by this time for a good meal in one of the fine restaurants in the area.

Glen Cove—Sea Cliff

Number of miles:	21 (short ride 13)
Approximate pedaling time:	3 hours (short ride 2 hours)
Terrain:	Hilly
Surface:	Good
Traffic:	Heavy in towns, moderate elsewhere
Things to see:	Garvies Point Museum and Preserve, East Island, St. John's Episcopal Church, Memorial Park (Sea Cliff)

Glen Cove dates from earliest colonial times, its first settlers appearing in the late 1600s. Because of its water access it grew as a thriving port and commercial center and became one of the major towns of Long Island. Sea Cliff dates from the mid-1800s when the heights south of Glen Cove, overlooking Hempstead Harbor, were used by a Methodist group as a summer meeting ground. The attractions of the area induced some of the group to build permanent residences, which in turn became the center of a popular summer resort community attracting visitors from New York City and elsewhere every year.

Glen Cove and Sea Cliff have, of course, changed dramatically since those days, Glen Cove especially having long since developed a busy urban environment. But traces of the past remain, the surrounding areas are still attractive, and the water view is as expansive as it has always been.

The ride begins at the Garvies Point Museum and Preserve in Glen Cove and proceeds north. Be ready for some hill climbing almost immediately. We enter estate country at New Woods Road and Dosoris Lane; on the right is a former Pratt Mansion (there were several Pratt family mansions in the area) now known as the Harrison House Conference Center. At the end of Dosoris Lane, if we go left,

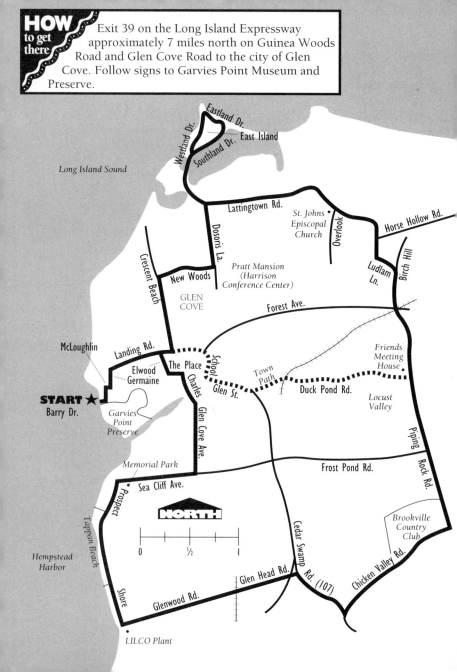

HOW to get there

Exit 39 on the Long Island Expressway approximately 7 miles north on Guinea Woods Road and Glen Cove Road to the city of Glen Cove. Follow signs to Garvies Point Museum and Preserve.

Eastland Dr.

Westland Dr.

East Island

Southland Dr.

Long Island Sound

Lattingtown Rd.

St. Johns Episcopal Church

Overlook

Horse Hollow Rd.

Dosoris La.

Crescent Beach

New Woods

Pratt Mansion (Harrison Conference Center)

Ludlam Ln.

Birch Hill

GLEN COVE

Forest Ave.

McLoughlin

Landing Rd.

Friends Meeting House

The Place

School St.

Town Path

Duck Pond Rd.

Elwood Germaine

Charles

Glen St.

Locust Valley

START ★
Barry Dr.

Garvies Point Preserve

Glen Cove Ave.

Piping Rock Rd.

Memorial Park

Frost Pond Rd.

Sea Cliff Ave.

Prospect

NORTH

0   ½   1

Hempstead Harbor

Tappan Beach

Cedar Swamp Rd. (107)

Brookville Country Club

Chicken Valley Rd.

Shore

Glenwood Rd.

Glen Head Rd.

LILCO Plant

**DIREC-
TIONS
at a glance**

- Start from Garvies Point Museum and Preserve. Go out of the parking lot onto Barry Drive for four blocks to McLoughlin Street.
- Right on McLoughlin Street half a block to Germaine Street.
- Left on Germaine Street one block to Landing Road.
- Right on Landing Road for about ¾ mile to Crescent Beach Road.
- Left on Crescent Beach Road for about 1 mile to New Woods Road on the right.
- Right on New Woods Road for about ¾ mile to its end at Dosoris Lane.
- Left on Dosoris Lane for approximately ¾ mile to its end at the Lattingtown Road intersection.
- Left at the intersection for a 2¾ mile circuit of East Island.
- Return to the Lattingtown Road-Dosoris Lane intersection and continue on Lattingtown Road for 2½ miles past St. John's Episcopal Church, to Ludlam Lane on the left.
- Left on Ludlam Lane to the merge with Birch Hill Road.
- Continue right on Birch Hill Road (which becomes Piping Rock Road) for 1¼ miles to Friends Meeting House at Duck Pond Road, then on for 2 miles to Chicken Valley Road. (Those taking the short ride go right on Duck Pond Road, over the railroad tracks, onto Town Path to Glen Street, right on Glen Street to School Street, then follow Garvies Point Museum signs back to the starting point.)
- Right on Chicken Valley Road past the Brookville Country Club ¾ miles to Cedar Swamp Road (Route 107).
- Right on Cedar Swamp Road to Glen Head Road on the left.
- Left on Glen Head Road, which becomes Glenwood Road just past the railroad tracks, down the long hill to Shore Avenue.
- Right at the Long Island Lighting Company plant on Shore Avenue, which becomes Prospect Avenue, for about 1¾ miles to Sea Cliff Avenue.
- Right on Sea Cliff Avenue for 1 mile to Glen Cove Avenue.

- Left on Glen Cove Avenue for about ¾ mile to Charles Street.
- Left on Charles Street to The Place, to Elwood, to Landing Road.
- Left on Landing Road to Germaine Street, McLoughlin Street, and Barry Drive back to the ride starting point.

---

we traverse two small causeways and come to East Island, the site of a former estate of J. P. Morgan. It is said that more than one hundred employees were required to tend the large mansion that once stood here and the supporting dairy and agricultural activities that Morgan instituted on the island. There are beautiful water views on the drives that ring the island.

Returning to Lattingtown Road we come to the Glen Cove Golf Course and Recreation Area and then pass estate grounds for a mile or so. This portion of the ride is exceptionally pleasant in midsummer when the road is shaded a cool green by the large overhanging trees. At the intersection of Lattingtown and Overlook roads is St. John's Episcopal Church of Lattingtown on the right, a beautiful stone structure comfortably settled into the hillside. Farther south we enter Locust Valley, containing some interesting antique stores and bookshops, where lunch can be obtained. Just south of here is Friends Meeting House, built in 1877, on the right at Piping Rock and Duck Pond roads.

Those taking the short ride turn right at this point toward Glen Cove via Duck Pond Road, Town Park, Glen Street, and School Street, and from there follow the markers back to Garvies Point Museum and Preserve. The main ride continues south along Piping Rock Road to Chicken Valley Road, passing the Brookville Country Club and attractive homes on beautifully treed acres. Cycle these roads with care since they are shoulderless and at times have heavy traffic.

At Glen Head Road the neighborhood changes abruptly to more conventional housing with the usual mix of stores and small businesses common to most of suburban Long Island. Glen Head Road is an uphill climb to a long downhill run to Glenwood Landing and Hempstead Harbor.

We go right at the giant Long Island Lighting Company generating plant, so out of place here, along Shore Road to Sea Cliff. Along the way is Tappan Beach where we get a good view across Hempstead Harbor of the Port Washington sand pits. At Sea Cliff we start an uphill climb on Prospect Avenue, continuing onto Sea Cliff Avenue. At the intersection of Sea Cliff and Prospect avenues is Memorial Park, a small patch of grass with a spectacular view of Long Island Sound, with Westchester visible on the horizon and Port Washington to the left. It is best to walk the half mile through Sea Cliff to observe closely its carefully maintained ornate "Carpenter Gothic Victorian" homes.

At Glen Cove Avenue we turn left and return to Glen Cove and Garvies Point Museum and Preserve. The half mile downhill on Glen Cove Avenue should be cycled with care since there is usually heavy and fast traffic. At the museum and preserve you might be interested in viewing the exhibits of regional geology and Indian archaeology, and if energy remains, in strolling the seventy-two acres of varied terrain and vegetation typical of Long Island.

Mill Neck—Center Island

Number of miles:	20 (short ride 10)
Approximate pedaling time:	3½ hours (short ride 2 hours)
Terrain:	Hilly
Surface:	Good; sandy in places
Traffic:	Moderate to heavy
Things to see:	Planting Fields Arboretum, Bailey Arboretum, Ransom Beach, Center Island, Seawanhaka Corinthian Yacht Club

The north shore of western Long Island is lined with enclosed bays, promontories, necks, and peninsulas on which many picturesque communities have developed. This ride explores some of the most interesting of these along an inland and water's-edge route through the villages of Mill Neck, Bayville, and Center Island. It traverses beautifully wooded areas and several beaches on Long Island Sound and Oyster Bay. The way is sometimes hilly, but the views are worth the effort.

The ride begins at the municipal parking lot in the village of Oyster Bay, on South Street, just north of East Main (Audrey Avenue) Street. We proceed out of the lot through the village, following signs to the Planting Fields Arboretum. Planting Fields, formerly the estate of W. R. Coe, features magnificent trees, a large collection of vines and shrubs, including an assemblage of rhododendrons and azaleas, and several tropical plant greenhouses.

From the arboretum we continue along Planting Fields Road west through Mill Neck. Mill Neck, like neighboring Matinecock and Locust Valley, is a heavily treed and hilly area and the site of many large and attractive homes. After an uphill climb on Oyster Bay Road,

HOW to get there

Exit 36 on Northern State Parkway, or Exit 43 on the Long Island Expressway, north on Oyster Bay Road about 2½ miles to the village of Syosset. Go through Syosset on Berry Hill Road for about 4 miles to South Street in Oyster Bay. Go right on South Street past East Main Street (Audrey Avenue) to the municipal parking lot indicated on the right.

Long Island Sound

Center Island Beach

Renaissance Health Spa

Ransom Beach

Bayville Ave.

BAYVILLE

Ludlam

West Harbor Dr.

CENTER ISLAND

Parking Lot Boat Ramps

Village Hall

Seawanhaka Rd.

Seawanhaka Corinthian Yacht Club

Bike Path

Bayville Rd.

Mill Neck Bay

Oyster Bay Harbor

Center Island Rd.

(Short Ride) Factory Pond

Horse Hollow Rd.

Bayville Rd.

West Shore Rd.

Bailey Arboretum

Feeks Ln.

Cleft Rd.

Oyster Bay Rd.

Frost Mill Rd.

MILL NECK

★ **START**

Audrey

West Main

East Main

Francis Pond

Planting Fields

Glen Cove

Mill Pond

Lexington

Mill River

South St.

OYSTER BAY

Planting Fields Arboretum

Berry Hill

To Syosset

Chicken Valley

NORTH

0   ½   1

DIREC-TIONS at a glance

- Start from the municipal parking lot on South Street in Oyster Bay. Left on South Street to West Main Street.
- Right on West Main Street to Lexington on the left.
- Left on Lexington to Mill River Road and sign indicating the way to the Planting Fields Arboretum.
- Right on Mill River Road about ½ mile to Glen Cove Road.
- Right on Glen Cove Road ½ mile to Planting Fields Road.
- Left on Planting Fields Road to the arboretum.
- Left (west) from the arboretum on Planting Fields Road to Chicken Valley Road.
- Right on Chicken Valley Road onto Oyster Bay Road, following sign to Locust Valley and the Bailey Arboretum.
- Continue on Oyster Bay Road over Francis Pond for about 1¾ miles to Bayville Road, just past the overpass.
- Right on Bayville Road, following signs to the Bailey Arboretum.
- Right from the arboretum on Bayville Road 1¾ miles to Bayville Avenue. A bike path exists for this segment north of Horse Hollow Road. (Those taking the short ride, turn right from Bayville Road onto Factory Pond Road about ¾ mile north of the arboretum. Continue on Factory Pond for about 1 mile to Feeks Lane [Cleft Road]. Left on Feeks Lane for 1¾ miles to West Shore Road. Right on West Shore onto West Main then South Street in Oyster Bay.)
- Proceed on Bayville Avenue past Ransom Beach, Ludlam Avenue, and Center Island Beach to the entrance to Center Island.
- Continue on Center Island Road for 2½ miles to the turnaround, then return. Seawanhaka Road and the Seawanhaka Corinthian Yacht Club are about halfway along.
- Go back on Bayville Avenue to West Harbor Drive, just past the Center Island Beach parking lot.
- Left on West Harbor Drive 1 mile to Ludlam Avenue.
- Left on Ludlam Avenue over bridge onto West Shore Road.

- Continue on West Shore Road for about 3 miles, under railroad overpass and past Mill Pond, onto West Main Street.
- Continue on West Main Street to South Street.
- Left on South Street to the municipal parking lot.

---

we go onto Bayville Road and come to Bailey Arboretum. For those who didn't get enough at Planting Fields, Bailey features a nineteenth-century house and a collection of rare plants.

From Bailey Arboretum we continue north on Bayville Road for a long downhill run into Bayville. (Those wishing to take a shorter ride can return to Oyster Bay through a hilly, but extremely pleasant, wooded area on Factory Pond Road and Feeks Lane [Cleft Road]. This also eliminates most of the heavily trafficked and narrow West Shore segment of the full ride.) The environment changes abruptly at Bayville from wooded hills to sandy seashore.

On the left is Ransom Beach on Long Island Sound. Opposite the beach is a string of restaurants and snack bars usually busy with beach patrons and cyclists.

Farther along on Bayville Avenue we proceed through a busier, crowded section. At one time this was primarily a summer vacation colony. It is fast becoming a year-round community, but most of the housing reflects its earlier use. We continue on Bayville Avenue past the Renaissance, a large health spa, straight through the Ludlam Avenue intersection and its perpetual traffic jam, and continue east. Traffic gets lighter past Ludlam Avenue as the neighborhood becomes less densely populated. After a mile or so we come to the Center Island Beach parking lot and boat launching ramps. The town beach straddles the peninsula and runs for ¾ mile to the entrance to the village of Center Island.

As the turnaround and police station at Center Island suggest, motorists are urged to turn at this point and head back to Bayville. Most cyclists, however, continue on Center Island Road, which runs for about 2½ miles into the peninsula. It is a beautiful shaded stretch, flanked by large homes and estates. About a mile along, on the left, is Seawanhaka Road, which runs past the Seawanhaka Corinthian Yacht

Club, one of the oldest and most prestigious yacht clubs in the United States, to Cold Spring Harbor. From here, on the right in the distance, is Cove Neck, the site of Theodore Roosevelt's estate, Sagamore Hill.

From Center Island we head back to Oyster Bay. We swing around Bayville on West Harbor Drive, heading for West Shore Road in Mill Neck. At the bridge leading to West Shore Road we get a beautiful view of Mill Neck Bay on the right and Oyster Bay Harbor on the left. The harbor view continues for the length of the ride on West Shore Road into Oyster Bay. Ride with care on this road since it is narrow and shoulderless and often has heavy traffic.

Oyster Bay—Brookville

Number of miles:	18 (short ride 13)
Approximate pedaling time:	4 hours (short ride 2½ hours)
Terrain:	Hilly
Surface:	Good; some sandy sections
Traffic:	Light to moderate
Things to see:	Nature Conservancy Preserve, Sagamore Hill, Theodore Roosevelt Memorial Sanctuary, Trailside Museum, Oyster Bay, Planting Fields Arboretum

It has been more than sixty years since Theodore Roosevelt lived at Sagamore Hill. Since that time the estate has been declared a National Historic Site and has become one of the major attractions of Long Island. It is the high point of this exceptionally scenic ride through the village of Oyster Bay and the adjoining villages of Brookville and Muttontown.

The village of Oyster Bay dates from colonial times and retains a decidedly early north shore flavor: a mix of New England colonial architecture, a salt-air environment, and hilly and heavily wooded terrain. Brookville and Muttontown, to the west and south of Oyster Bay, are large wooded tracts dotted with estates and fine old homes. The countryside is covered with stands of towering graceful trees, which during summer make every road a delightfully cool tunnel of mixed sunlight and shade. Because of the beauty of the area, and its challenging terrain, it is a favorite with cyclists.

The ride starts from the Syosset railroad-station parking lot, heading east onto Cold Spring Road to Route 25A. We loop west on Route 25A and proceed for about a mile to Cove Road. Turning right at

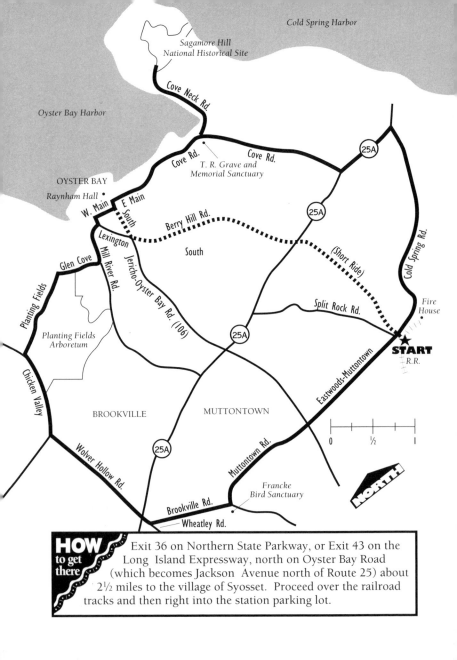

Cold Spring Harbor

Sagamore Hill
National Historical Site

Cove Neck Rd.

Oyster Bay Harbor

Cove Rd.

Cove Rd.

25A

T. R. Grave and
Memorial Sanctuary

OYSTER BAY

Raynham Hall •

E Main

25A

Cold Spring Rd.

W. Main

South

Berry Hill Rd.

Lexington

South

(Short Ride)

Glen Cove

Mill River Rd.

Jericho-Oyster Bay Rd. (106)

Split Rock Rd.

Fire
House

Planting Fields

Planting Fields
Arboretum

25A

START
R.R.

Chicken Valley

Eastwoods-Muttontown

BROOKVILLE

MUTTONTOWN

0   ½   1

Wolver Hollow Rd.

25A

Muttontown Rd.

NORTH

Francke
Bird Sanctuary

Brookville Rd.

Wheatley Rd.

HOW to get there Exit 36 on Northern State Parkway, or Exit 43 on the Long Island Expressway, north on Oyster Bay Road (which becomes Jackson Avenue north of Route 25) about 2½ miles to the village of Syosset. Proceed over the railroad tracks and then right into the station parking lot.

- Start from the Syosset railroad-station parking lot. Proceed to Cold Spring Road at the end of the lot near the firehouse.
- Right on Cold Spring Road, following the sign to Cold Spring Harbor, for about 3 miles to Route 25A.
- Left on Route 25A for 1 mile to Cove Road and sign indicating Sagamore Hill.
- Right at the sign onto Cove Road for approximately 1¾ miles to Sagamore Hill, then return to the Theodore Roosevelt Memorial Sanctuary.
- Left from the grave site (or right from Sagamore Hill) on Cove Road (later East Main Street) toward the village of Oyster Bay.
- Continue on East Main Street past Oyster Bay High School, Christ Episcopal Church, and First Presbyterian Church, to South Street.
- Left on South Street to West Main Street. (For the short ride, proceed about ½ mile up South Street to Berry Hill Road. Go left on Berry Hill for about 4 miles to Eastwoods-Muttontown Road and left to the station parking lot in Syosset.)
- Right on West Main Street past Raynham Hall to Lexington.
- Left on Lexington to Mill River Road and a sign indicating the way to the Planting Fields Arboretum.
- Right on Mill River Road about ½ mile to Glen Cove Road.
- Right on Glen Cove Road to Planting Fields Road.
- Left on Planting Fields Road to the gate of the arboretum.
- Left (west) from the arboretum on Planting Fields Road to Chicken Valley Road.
- Left on Chicken Valley Road to Wolver Hollow Road.
- Left on Wolver Hollow Road for about 1¾ miles through upper Brookville, across Route 25A onto Brookville Road, bearing left at the fork with Wheatley Road.
- Continue on Brookville Road for about 1¼ miles to Muttontown Road, opposite the Jane B. Francke bird sanctuary.

- Left on Muttontown Road through Muttontown for about 1½ miles to Route 106, Jericho-Oyster Bay Road.
- Continue across Route 106 onto Eastwoods-Muttontown Road for about 1½ miles across Split Rock Road in Syosset, onto Cold Spring Road to the railroad parking lot.

Cove Road we begin a smooth gentle downhill run through the beginning of an area of large homes and estates. Turning right at the sign for Sagamore Hill, at Cove Road, we obtain our first view of Oyster Bay Harbor, a wide expanse of blue water flecked with small sailboats and powerboats. Cycle with care here since Cove Road is narrow and shoulderless. Beyond it is the village of Oyster Bay. We turn right at the sign for Sagamore Hill and come to a steep hill indeed. Be prepared to walk up this stretch.

Sagamore Hill is always a pleasure to visit. The house, built in 1885, exudes an aura of warmth and comfort, the simply landscaped grounds are spacious and well tended, and there is a grand view of the harbor and Long Island Sound. The site also features the Old Orchard Museum, built in 1938, the former home of Roosevelt's son, Theodore Roosevelt, Jr.

From Sagamore Hill, we return to Cove Road and the Roosevelt grave site and, next to it, the Theodore Roosevelt Memorial Sanctuary and Trailside Museum, owned by the National Audubon Society. The grave site is simple and quiet, the sanctuary offers twelve acres of undisturbed land containing a variety of trees and bird species, and the museum displays numerous Long Island plants and animals. The trails are open to society members only.

From here we proceed to the village of Oyster Bay. The road is lined with new and old homes of Victorian and other nineteenth-century styles, with an estate here and there. On East Main Street we pass Oyster Bay High School, a huge brick structure, Christ Episcopal Church on the right, and the First Presbyterian Church on the left. The Episcopal church, a slate-roofed stone structure, dates from 1879 and was attended by Roosevelt for many years; the Presbyterian

Church is an interesting example of Carpenter Gothic on a large scale. On West Main Street is Raynham Hall, a gray saltbox home dating from 1738, where British forces maintained quarters during the Revolutionary War. All along East and West Main streets are interesting Victorian and even older homes.

From Oyster Bay, those taking the short ride proceed south on South Street to Berry Hill Road, following this all the way back to Syosset. The full ride continues on to Planting Fields Arboretum. Planting Fields, the former estate of W. R. Coe, features hundreds of acres of trees and shrubs on wide lawns, an extensive collection of rhododendrons and azaleas, and a number of greenhouses with collections of tropical plants.

The remainder of the ride route goes through Upper Brookville and Muttontown, along 7 miles of rather narrow and shoulderless but always scenic roads back to Syosset. Country clubs, estates, and large homes abound on all sides. Just past the Woodcrest Club we reenter Syosset, the ride starting point.

Huntington—Lloyd Neck

Number of miles:	19 (8½ without Lloyd Neck)
Approximate pedaling time:	4 hours (2 hours without Lloyd Neck)
Terrain:	Hilly
Surface:	Good; some sandy sections
Traffic:	Heavy in Huntington and Cold Spring Harbor, moderate elsewhere
Things to see:	Huntington Harbor, Coindre Hall, Henry Lloyd Manor House, Black Oak Tree, Target Rock National Wildlife Refuge, Cold Spring Harbor Whaling Museum

Huntington and Lloyd Neck make up one of the several peninsulas that jut into Long Island Sound on Long Island's north shore. It is a charming and picturesque area that is rich in colonial history and architecture while offering superb water views.

The ride heads north from Huntington Village toward Huntington Harbor. From West Shore Road we get a continuous view of the harbor and, in the early morning, hours the hundreds of small sailboats and pleasure craft moored chock-a-block on its surface. In good sailing weather it's interesting to watch the feats of seamanship performed by these squadrons as they maneuver to reach Long Island Sound simultaneously.

At Browns Road we start a ½ mile uphill climb that can be relieved somewhat by a stop at Coindre Hall, a large French Norman–style building built around 1915 as a residence for George McKesson Brown, a New York drug manufacturer. Since the 1930s it has been used variously as a Catholic school for boys, a county-run art center and school, and an archaeological museum. Looking east from the

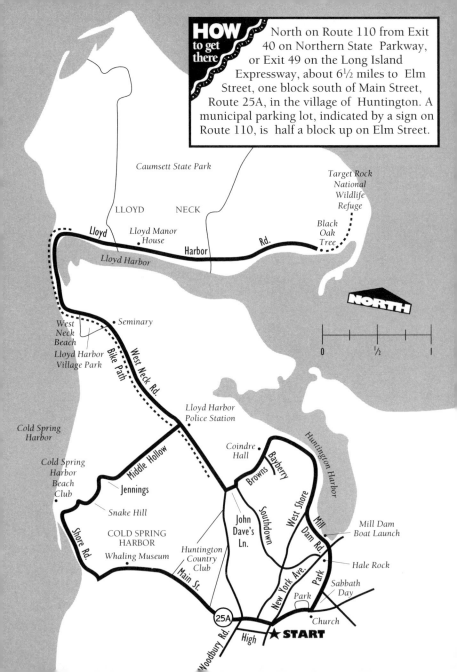

HOW to get there

North on Route 110 from Exit 40 on Northern State Parkway, or Exit 49 on the Long Island Expressway, about 6½ miles to Elm Street, one block south of Main Street, Route 25A, in the village of Huntington. A municipal parking lot, indicated by a sign on Route 110, is half a block up on Elm Street.

Caumsett State Park

Target Rock National Wildlife Refuge

LLOYD   NECK

Black Oak Tree

Lloyd

Lloyd Manor House

Harbor   Rd.

Lloyd Harbor

NORTH

0   ½   1

West Neck Beach

Seminary

Lloyd Harbor Village Park

Bike Path

West Neck Rd.

Cold Spring Harbor

Lloyd Harbor Police Station

Coindre Hall

Baxberry

Huntington Harbor

Cold Spring Harbor Beach Club

Middle Hollow

Browns

Jennings

Southdown

West Shore

Mill Dam Boat Launch

Snake Hill

John Dave's Ln.

Mill

COLD SPRING HARBOR

Dam Rd.

Hale Rock

Shore Rd.

Whaling Museum

Huntington Country Club

Main St.

New York Ave.

Park

Sabbath Day

Park

Church

25A

Woodbury Rd.   High   ★ START

DIREC-TIONS at a glance

- The ride starts at the municipal parking lot on Elm Street, one block south of Main Street (Route 25A) in Huntington.
- Proceed out of the parking lot onto Elm Street and then right to New York Avenue, then right again to Main Street.
- Right on Main Street about ½ mile to Sabbath Day Path on the left, just past the Old First Presbyterian Church.
- Left on Sabbath Day Path to merge with Park Avenue on the right. Continue left on Park about ½ mile to merge with New York Avenue and the intersection with Mill Dam Road at Nathan Hale Rock.
- Left on Mill Dam Road at the head of Huntington Harbor about ½ mile to West Shore Road.
- Right on West Shore Road about 1 mile onto Browns Road.
- Continue on Browns Road to Coindre Hall opposite Bayberry Lane, then on to Southdown Road.
- Jog left on Southdown Road to John Dave's Lane on the right.
- Right on John Dave's Lane to West Neck Road.
- Right on West Neck Road, following bike-route signs for about 3¼ miles to Lloyd Neck and Lloyd Harbor Road. The Seminary of the Immaculate Conception is on the right.
- Continue on Lloyd Harbor Road (no bike path), passing Caumsett State Park and Lloyd Manor House, for about 2½ miles to its end, at the Black Oak Tree and Target Rock National Wildlife Refuge.
- Return on Lloyd Harbor Road and West Neck Road to Middle Hollow Road on the right, opposite the police station.
- Right on Middle Hollow Road to its end at Jennings Road.
- Right on Jennings Road for about ¼ mile, following the yellow traffic divider left onto Snake Hill Road, then on for about ¾ mile downhill to its end at Shore Road.
- Left on Shore Road for about ¾ mile to Main Street (Route 25A) in Cold Spring Harbor.

- Left on Main Street to the Whaling Museum, then on, following Route 25A signs, 1½ miles back to New York Avenue (Route 110) in Huntington.
- Right on New York Avenue to the Elm Street municipal parking lot and starting point of the ride.

rear of the building, past the old estate boathouse at the water's edge, we have a stunning view of Huntington Harbor and its outlet to Long Island Sound at Sandy Point.

From Browns Road we continue north along West Neck Road on the Lloyd Harbor bike path, through an attractive wooded area of fine new homes and several well-preserved Victorian- and colonial-style structures. Opposite Lloyd Harbor Village Park is the Seminary of the Immaculate Conception of the Roman Catholic Diocese of Brooklyn. The grounds are closed to the public, but from the entry road on West Neck Road you can get a good view of the impressive brick Italianate structure in a parklike setting that forms the nucleus of the seminary.

Just past West Neck Beach the path runs on a narrow isthmus to Lloyd Harbor Road on Lloyd Neck. The bike path ends at this point. Lloyd Harbor Road has some traffic and is hilly and narrow, but it's a scenic stretch going through lightly developed woods, with Lloyd Harbor sparkling through the foliage.

Along this road we find the Joseph Lloyd House, a stately white clapboard colonial structure dating from 1760, and just farther on, the original Henry Lloyd Manor House, a more modest shingled saltbox structure dating from 1711. Just east of these is the entrance to Caumsett State Park, a former estate of Marshall Field. Its 1,500 acres offer miles of bike paths and terrific Long Island Sound views. At the very end of Lloyd Harbor Road is the famous Black Oak Tree, said to be the largest black oak in the United States (20 feet in circumference; 100 feet tall; 150-foot branch spread). Past the Black Oak Tree, up the road, is the Target Rock National Wildlife Refuge. The preserve contains formal gardens and trails through typical Long Island landforms and vegetation.

Retracing our way from Lloyd Neck on West Neck Road, we come to Middle Hollow Road and start a long uphill trek to Jennings Road. From here we begin a long, steep, twisting descent on aptly named Snake Hill Road. Be sure to check your brakes before starting down this exhilarating stretch. At the bottom we come to Shore Road and the Cold Spring Harbor Beach Club.

Continuing south on Shore Road we turn left on heavily traveled Main Street (Route 25A) in Cold Spring Harbor and pass charming Victorian and colonial homes and shops that recapture the country village atmosphere that existed here a century ago. The buildings now house fine boutiques, craft shops, and restaurants. On the left on the way back to Huntington is the Cold Spring Harbor Whaling Museum, featuring a plethora of displays on whaling as it was once practiced. After one last hill climb on Main Street, we pass the Huntington Country Club and return to Huntington Village and the ride starting point.

Northport—Eaton's Neck

Number of miles:	17 (6½ without Eaton's Neck)
Approximate pedaling time:	3½ hours (1½ hours without Eaton's Neck)
Terrain:	Hilly (with narrow roads on Eaton's Neck)
Surface:	Good; some sandy sections
Traffic:	Heavy in Northport, moderate elsewhere
Things to see:	Bayview Avenue, beaches, Northport Harbor

Northport is a pleasant old village nestled some distance north of the main traffic arteries of the north shore. It is located at the base of Eaton's Neck peninsula, which juts out 3 miles into Long Island Sound. English and New England settlers first arrived here in the 1600s, and in time the village became a major boatbuilding and oystering center. Northport and Eaton's Neck peninsula offer a most interesting ride because of the combination of historical atmosphere, magnificent water views, and varied terrain found in few other places on Long Island.

The ride starts from the parking lot at the foot of Main Street on Northport Harbor. It proceeds north on charming Bayview Avenue, lined with nineteenth-century homes, to James Street. James Street is a difficult steep hill climb and is best walked. All along James Street and Ocean Avenue, which follows it, however, is a terrific view of Northport Bay and Eaton's Neck to the north. On clear days the Connecticut hills are visible on the horizon. Unfortunately there is also an unobstructed view of the Long Island Lighting Company's four-stack Northport electric generating plant, a mass of steel and concrete completely at odds with its surroundings.

Continuing north on Eaton's Neck Road we go down from the

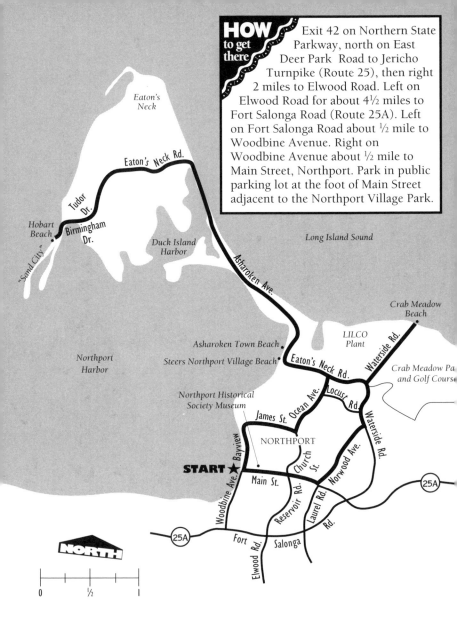

HOW
to get
there

Exit 42 on Northern State Parkway, north on East Deer Park Road to Jericho Turnpike (Route 25), then right 2 miles to Elwood Road. Left on Elwood Road for about 4½ miles to Fort Salonga Road (Route 25A). Left on Fort Salonga Road about ½ mile to Woodbine Avenue. Right on Woodbine Avenue about ½ mile to Main Street, Northport. Park in public parking lot at the foot of Main Street adjacent to the Northport Village Park.

Eaton's Neck

Eaton's Neck Rd.

Tudor Dr.

Hobart Beach

Birmingham Dr.

"Sand City"

Duck Island Harbor

Long Island Sound

Asharoken Ave.

Crab Meadow Beach

LILCO Plant

Waterside Rd.

Asharoken Town Beach

Steers Northport Village Beach

Eaton's Neck Rd.

Crab Meadow Park and Golf Course

Northport Harbor

Northport Historical Society Museum

James St.

Ocean Ave.

Locust Rd.

Waterside Rd.

NORTHPORT

Church St.

Norwood Ave.

START ★

Bayview

Main St.

Woodbine Ave.

Reservoir Rd.

Laurel Rd.

Rd.

25A

25A

Fort Salonga

Elwood Rd.

NORTH

0   ½   1

DIREC- TIONS at a glance

- Start from the public parking lot at the foot of Main Street on Northport Harbor.
- Go left from Main Street on Bayview Avenue about ½ mile to its end at James Street.
- Right on James Street ½ mile uphill to Ocean Avenue.
- Left on Ocean Avenue about ½ mile to Eaton's Neck Road.
- Left on Eaton's Neck Road about ½ mile downhill past Steers Northport Village Beach and then Asharoken Beach onto Asharoken Avenue.
- Continue about 3 miles on Asharoken Avenue on narrow isthmus to Eaton's Neck Road in village of Eaton's Neck.
- Continue on Eaton's Neck Road for about 1 mile, to Tudor Drive on the right.
- Right on Tudor Drive (following beach signs) to Worcester Drive to Birmingham Drive and on to Hobart Town Beach.
- Return to Northport via Birmingham, Worcester, Tudor, Eaton's Neck Road, Asharoken Avenue, and Eaton's Neck Road, going past Ocean Avenue to Waterside Road on the left, past the LILCO plant entrance road.
- Left on Waterside about 1 mile, with Crab Meadow Park and Golf Course on the right, to Crab Meadow Beach.
- Return on Waterside, going left past Eaton's Neck Road, continuing on Waterside for about ½ mile to Norwood Avenue on the right.
- Right on Norwood Avenue for about 1 mile to Main Street.
- Right on Main Street, past the Northport Historical Society Museum, to its end at Northport Harbor and the ride starting point.

heights of Ocean Avenue to the Asharoken isthmus, which connects Northport to Eaton's Neck. As we enter the village of Asharoken we pass Steers Northport Village Beach and, adjoining it, Asharoken Beach. From here we continue on Asharoken Avenue on the narrow strip of beach that separates Long Island Sound from Northport Bay. At points the isthmus is no more than 150 feet wide, with an abrupt drop-off to the sound on the right and comfortable summer cottages and homes on the left. This is a difficult stretch for cyclists since the road is shoulderless and extremely narrow.

As we progress into Eaton's Neck the terrain abruptly changes from flat sandy shore to wooded hills. We continue on these ups and downs through Eaton's Neck, following the signs indicating the way to the town beach. After passing through a community of neat, modern homes we come to Hobart Beach at the end of the road. This is a good place to rest, and swim if you like, or just enjoy the views— Long Island Sound to the north, Lloyd Neck to the west, and a pleasant small boat-filled harbor to the south. Stretching out into Northport Harbor from Hobart Beach is a two-pronged peninsula known as "Sand City." There are no roads on it, and so it is an uncrowded swimming beach area where pleasure boaters often anchor.

Returning, we trace our way back through Eaton's Neck to the narrow strip of Asharoken Avenue and head back toward Northport, squarely facing the omnipresent stacks of the generating plant. We get an even closer view of these as we go past the plant on Eaton's Neck Road. Although the plant is an eyesore, it provides a vital service, producing about one-third of the electric energy used on Long Island.

As we head north on Waterside Avenue, we pass the Crab Meadow Park and Golf Course, with its manicured greens and stately trees, and arrive at Crab Meadow Beach. It has a small snack bar in an attractive sand-colored cement and stucco beach house, complete with red-tiled roof, at which you can get hot dogs, hamburgers, and soft drinks.

From Crab Meadow Beach we head back on Waterside Avenue to Norwood Road and the center of Northport village. At the intersection of Main Street and Woodside Avenue is the Northport Historical Society Museum, featuring items of historical interest on Northport and its environs and offering a detailed walking guide of the village. It is worthwhile to obtain this pamphlet and explore on foot the dozens of homes, commercial establishments, and stores dating from the early 1800s that line Main Street and Bayview and Woodbine avenues along Northport Harbor.

Smithtown—Nissequogue

Number of miles:	12
Approximate pedaling time:	3 hours
Terrain:	Hilly
Surface:	Good; some sandy sections
Traffic:	Moderate to heavy
Things to see:	"Bull" Smythe monument, St. James General Store, Old Nissequogue School, Village of the Branch

The town of Smithtown originally existed as a privately owned duchy of the Smythe family, stretching from the Long Island Sound to Islip and from Huntington to Setauket. Richard "Bull" Smythe, so-called because of his purported proclivity for bull riding, obtained the land from the Gardiner family (of Gardiner's Island) in 1663. Tradition has it that the western boundary of the property was established by Smythe's agreement with the Matinecock Indians of the north shore that in exchange for some (unknown) consideration, Smythe would be allowed all the land he could circumscribe in one day's bull riding. The legend is commemorated in the famous bronze bull monument at the intersection of Routes 25 and 25A in Smithtown.

The terrain of eastern Smithtown and the Nissequogue peninsula varies from wooded hills to the beachfront of Long Island Sound and wetlands of the Nissequogue River. This is a relatively difficult ride, however, since all the roads in the area, while very scenic, are narrow and shoulderless and offer little forward visibility. The ride starts from the Village of the Branch and proceeds north on North Country Road (Route 25A). This is a gradual uphill climb with appreciable traffic but with a wide shoulder. Off North Country Road, at the end of Harbor Hill Road at Moriches Road, is the St. James General Store

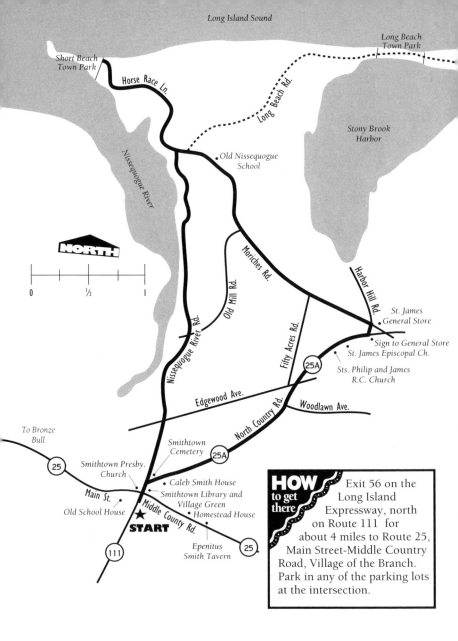

Long Island Sound

Short Beach
Town Park

Long Beach
Town Park

Horse Race Ln.

Long Beach Rd.

Stony Brook
Harbor

Nissequogue River

Old Nissequogue
School

NORTH

0   ½   1

Moriches Rd.

Old Mill Rd.

Nissequogue River Rd.

Fifty Acres Rd.

Harbor Hill Rd.

St. James
General Store

Sign to General Store
St. James Episcopal Ch.

25A

Sts. Philip and James
R.C. Church

Edgewood Ave.

North Country Rd.

Woodlawn Ave.

To Bronze
Bull

25

Smithtown
Cemetery

25A

Smithtown Presby.
Church

Main St.

Old School House

Caleb Smith House

Smithtown Library and
Village Green

Middle County Rd.

★ START

Homestead House

111

Epenitus
Smith Tavern

25

HOW
to get
there

Exit 56 on the
Long Island
Expressway, north
on Route 111 for
about 4 miles to Route 25,
Main Street-Middle Country
Road, Village of the Branch.
Park in any of the parking lots
at the intersection.

DIREC-TIONS at a glance

- Start from any of the parking lots at the intersection of Route 111 and Main Street-Middle Country Road (Route 25) in Village of the Branch.
- Proceed north across Middle Country Road, bearing right past the Smithtown Library onto Route 25A, North Country Road.
- Continue on North Country Road for about 2¾ miles, past Sts. Philip and James Church, and St. James Episcopal Church to Harbor Hill Road on the left.
- Left on Harbor Hill Road 1 block to Moriches Road and the General Store.
- Left on Moriches Road for about 3 miles to Horse Race Lane, passing the Old Nissequogue School on the right. Follow Horse Race Lane for about 1 mile to Short Beach. (About ½ mile past the schoolhouse is Long Beach Road on the right, a 5½-mile round-trip to Long Beach Park on the Nissequogue Peninsula.)
- Return from Short Beach on Horse Race Lane to Nissequogue River Road on the right.
- Right on Nissequogue River Road for about 3¼ miles to Middle Country Road and Route 111, the ride starting point.

and Drug Museum. The store has been here since 1857 and offers an assortment of handcrafted knickknacks.

Proceeding north on Moriches Road, which is shoulderless and quite narrow, we enter the village of Nissequogue, passing fine old Victorian and colonial homes in a semirural setting, with stretches of farmland and open fields. Nissequogue was probably the most desirable of the Smythe family holdings since it was here that the original Smythe homestead was established. On the right is the Old Nissequogue School, built in 1808 by seven members of the Smythe clan and one Peter Jayne.

Just past the schoolhouse is Long Beach Road, a 5½-mile run through beautifully wooded land dotted with attractive homes and several horse farms. This peninsula is said to have been the headquarters location of the Nissequogue Indians, the original owners of the land. It was later farmed successfully by the earliest Smythe family settlers and their descendants. Along the way is Long Beach Town Park on Long Island Sound. At the peninsula's end is a private yacht club from which you can enjoy an excellent view of Stony Brook Harbor.

Returning from Long Beach, we proceed north on Horse Race Lane to Short Beach Town Park, past which the Nissequogue River empties into Long Island Sound. There is swimming available on wide pleasant beaches, and a small snack shop offers sandwiches, coffee, hot dogs, and other goodies. The approach to the beach offers an excellent view of the Nissequogue River. The shores are tidal flats in which a large variety of waterfowl and marsh vegetation can be seen. Across the way are the buildings of the King's Park State Hospital.

From Short Beach we return south on Nissequogue River Road. All along the way on this rather hilly but scenic road are well-tended, spacious, and attractive homes. On the right bordering the road is the gradually narrowing Nissequogue River.

At the end of this leg we come back to the ride starting point in the Village of the Branch. It is interesting to explore on foot the colonial homes and buildings that have been maintained in the village. These include the Caleb Smith House (c. 1819) on North Country Road just past the Smithtown Library; the Homestead House (c. 1768) and Epenitus Smith Tavern (c. 1750) just east of the library; the Smithtown Presbyterian Church (c. 1750) opposite the library; and the Old School House (c. 1802) on Singer Avenue south of Main Street. At the intersection of North Country Road and Nissequogue River Road is the Smithtown Cemetery, in which many Smythe family descendants are buried.

Stony Brook—
Port Jefferson

Number of miles:	17 (11 without Port Jefferson segment)
Approximate pedaling time:	4 hours (3 hours without Port Jefferson segment)
Terrain:	Hilly
Surface:	Generally good; some sections rough surfaced and sandy
Traffic:	Heavy on Route 25A and Port Jefferson, light to moderate elsewhere
Things to see:	Old Stone Lighthouse, Melville Memorial Park, Brewster House, Port Jefferson Harbor, Thompson House, Barn Complex, Stony Brook Museums

Stony Brook, Setauket, and Port Jefferson are old colonial communities dating from the mid-1600s, when Setauket, settled by New Englanders, became the first community in what was to become the town of Brookhaven. The area remains as it must have been then—wooded hills, scenic and inviting harbors, and permeating it all a feeling of prosperity and comfort. The ride begins at Stony Brook Harbor, proceeds east through Setauket and Port Jefferson, and returns to Stony Brook. It is recommended that some additional time be allotted at the end of the ride to allow for a stroll through the interesting museum complex at Stony Brook.

We leave Stony Brook and head for Old Field Point. Christian Avenue is a long uphill climb along which are interesting colonial-style homes on pleasant, tree-shaded grounds. On Quaker Path the surroundings become more rural and the trees and houses larger. Finally, on Old Field Road we go through an area of extremely attractive homes on spacious and well-tended acres. At Old Field Point, from

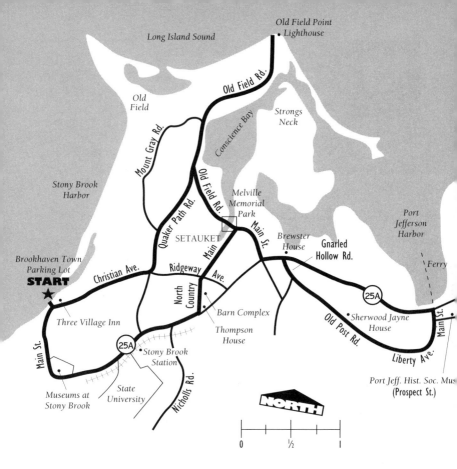

Old Field Point
• Lighthouse

Long Island Sound

Old Field Rd.

Old
Field

Strongs
Neck

Conscience Bay

Mount Gray Rd.

Stony Brook
Harbor

Old Field Rd.

Melville
Memorial
Park

Port
Jefferson
Harbor

Quaker Path Rd.

SETAUKET

Main

Main St.

Brewster
House

Gnarled
Hollow Rd.

Ferry

Brookhaven Town
Parking Lot
START

Christian Ave.

Ridgeway

Ave.

North
Country

Barn Complex

25A

Sherwood Jayne
House

Three Village Inn

Thompson
House

Old Post Rd.

Main St.

25A

Stony Brook
Station

Museums at
Stony Brook

State
University

Nicholls Rd.

Liberty Ave.

Main St.

Port Jeff. Hist. Soc. Mus
(Prospect St.)

NORTH

0   ½   1

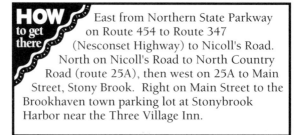

HOW
to get
there
East from Northern State Parkway
on Route 454 to Route 347
(Nesconset Highway) to Nicoll's Road.
North on Nicoll's Road to North Country
Road (route 25A), then west on 25A to Main
Street, Stony Brook. Right on Main Street to the
Brookhaven town parking lot at Stonybrook
Harbor near the Three Village Inn.

- Start from the Brookhaven town parking lot at Stony Brook Harbor near the Three Village Inn.
- Proceed around the circle onto Main, then left onto Christian Avenue.
- Continue on Christian Avenue for about 1¾ miles to Quaker Path.
- Left on Quaker Path for about 1 mile to Old Field Road.
- Left on Old Field Road for about 2 miles to Old Field Point.
- Return from Old Field Point about 3½ miles on Old Field Road onto Main Street in Setauket, to Route 25A.
- Left on Route 25A for about 3½ miles to Main Street (Route 112) in Port Jefferson.
- Right on Main Street ¼ mile to Liberty Avenue on the right.
- Right on Liberty Avenue one block, then straight ahead onto Old Post Road for about 2 miles to its end at Gnarled Hollow Road.
- Right on Gnarled Hollow Road about ¼ mile to Route 25A.
- Left on 25A for about ¼ mile to Main Street on the right.
- Right on Main Street to Melville Memorial Park at the head of Conscience Bay.
- Continue on Main Street and North Country Road, left at the bridge, back to 25A.
- Right on Route 25A for about 3½ miles to Main Street in Stony Brook, near the Museums at Stony Brook complex.
- Right on Main Street about ½ mile back to the ride starting point.

the edge of a sand cliff that drops off steeply to the water, we obtain a grand view of Long Island Sound with Connecticut in the distance. To the right is the Old Stone Lighthouse, built in 1868, now a private residence.

Returning to Old Field Road we see Conscience Bay on the left, presenting a serene waterscape complete with substantial bayside homes and attractive sailboats gliding lazily along. Farther on we come to the village of Setauket. This is the oldest village in the area and once served as the seat of local government. Its importance derived in its location at the head of Conscience Bay at the confluence of two streams that entered the bay at this point. As in so many other places, the mills set up on the streams became the center of commerce and public activity. At the head of Conscience Bay currently is Melville Memorial Park, containing an upper and lower mill pond and an old mill and post office.

At the end of Main Street in Setauket we come to heavily trafficked Route 25A, which we follow all the way to Port Jefferson. On the left, three blocks from Main Street on Runs Road, is the Brewster House, a restored early-eighteenth-century home. At the end of the long downhill run is the waterfront area of Port Jefferson, a place completely different in pace from the serenity of Setauket and Stony Brook. Here all is hustle and bustle, with heavy traffic and crowded streets. Autos and people depart for Bridgeport, Connecticut, on ferries leaving from the foot of Main Street. Boat horns sound and motorboats roar. This contrast must always have existed, since from its earliest days Port Jefferson was an important north shore harbor. It was an early center of shipbuilding and a landing from which cordwood, taken from the pine and oak barrens to the south in the middle of the island, was shipped to New York. On Prospect Street is the Port Jefferson Historical Society Museum, in which mementos of the village's vibrant past are displayed.

We return toward Setauket on Old Post Road, past the Sherwood-Jayne House, built around 1730, in which can be seen antique home furnishings and craft items. We continue west on Route 25A to Main Street, which loops north to Conscience Bay from 25A at this point and then returns south to North Country Road. On North Country Road is the Thompson House, an early-eighteenth-century farmhouse, currently the headquarters of the Society for the Preservation of Long Island Antiquities. Just north of this is the Barn Complex, a restored eighteenth-century barn displaying typical farming equipment of the time.

We continue south on North Country Road to 25A, then west (right) on 25A past the Stony Brook railroad station, out to Main Street in Stony Brook. You can walk the remaining ½ mile to better peruse the Museums at Stony Brook.

Wading River

Number of miles:	18 (9 miles without farm segment)
Approximate pedaling time:	4 hours
Terrain:	Hilly near Wading River and shore, flat elsewhere
Surface:	Generally good; some sections rough-surfaced and sandy
Traffic:	Light to moderate
Things to see:	Wading River, Shoreham Nuclear Power Plant, Miller Homestead, Wildwood State Park

Long Island was shaped by ancient glaciers that scoured New England and scraped out Long Island Sound. The most visible remains of this action are the sand bluffs bordering the Sound from Port Jefferson to Orient Point and the hilly moraines that line the island along its north shore and middle. The hills provided the most attractive areas for settlements, and their loamy soil proved excellent for farming. This ride explores one of the oldest of such communities and goes through farmlands that lie on the gentle slopes back from the edges of the bluffs.

The ride begins at Wildwood State Park and proceeds onto North Wading River Road, heading west toward Wading River. The road is quite hilly and at points may have to be walked. It is attractive, however, lined with heavy woods and neat, comfortable-looking homes. We turn north on North Side Road just past the Little Flower Institute, a Catholic home for orphaned and disadvantaged children, and continue on hilly terrain to Sound Road and Wading River Town Beach.

At the beach we can see the sand bluffs stretching away in both directions and the giant boulders deposited here and there by the glaciers. The bluffs are imposing but fragile, with those sections unprotected by vegetative cover gradually being eaten away by the ac-

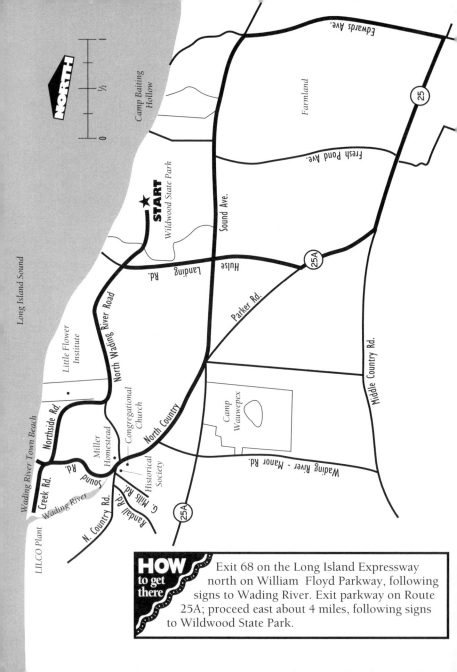

Long Island Sound

Camp Baiting Hollow

Edwards Ave.

Farmland

25

Fresh Pond Ave.

Sound Ave.

Wildwood State Park

★ START

25A

Landing Rd.

Hulse

Parker Rd.

North Wading River Road

Little Flower Institute

Wading River Town Beach

Northside Rd.

Congregational Church

Miller Homestead

North Country

Camp Wauwepex

Middle Country Rd.

Creek Rd.

Sound Rd.

N. Country Rd.

Randall Rd.

G. Mills Rd.

Historical Society

Wading River

25A

Wading River - Manor Rd.

LILCO Plant

NORTH

0   ½   1

HOW to get there Exit 68 on the Long Island Expressway north on William Floyd Parkway, following signs to Wading River. Exit parkway on Route 25A; proceed east about 4 miles, following signs to Wildwood State Park.

- From the Wildwood State Park parking lot, proceed west toward Wading River on North Wading River Road about 1¾ miles to North Side Road, just past Little Flower Institute.
- Right on North Side Road about 1 mile to Sound Road.
- Right on Sound Road to Wading River Town Beach.
- From Wading River Town Beach continue on Creek Road to its end at the Wading River outlet on Long Island Sound.
- Return on Creek Road to Sound Road, then right on Sound Road for about ½ mile to North Country Road in the town of Wading River.
- Left through the town past the Historical Society, Congregational Church, and Miller Homestead on North Country Road for about 1¼ miles, to the intersection with Sound Avenue and Route 25A. Note that North Country Road goes left at Wading River Manor Road.
- Proceed left on Sound Avenue about 3½ miles to Edwards Avenue.
- Right on Edwards Avenue about 2 miles to Route 25, Middle Country Road. Be prepared for a steep hill and gully at Baiting Hollow.
- Right on Route 25 about 3 miles, bearing right onto Route 25A. Follow signs to Wildwood State Park, until you reach Hulse Landing Road.
- Right on Hulse Landing Road about 2 miles to Wildwood State Park and the ride starting point.

tion of tides and storms. Directly behind Creek Road, lined with beachfront cottages, are the flat and marshy Wading River wetlands. The river itself can be seen at the end of Creek Road, emptying into Long Island Sound. There is a boat-launching ramp here and usually a good deal of activity as fishers and water-skiers come and go. The river at low flow is a slow-moving, shallow trickle; after heavy rains, however, it's a swift, strong stream. Just beyond the river is the Long Island Lighting Company's (LILCO) Shoreham electric generating plant, a planned atomic-powered facility that has permanently altered the rustic atmosphere of the area. The plant, construction of which began in the early 1970s, was completed in the early 1990s and during that period was the subject of claim and counterclaim by power advocates and environmentalists. Finally, in the face of ever increasing opposition to its operation, the plant was sold by LILCO to New York State, which in turn had it decommissioned. This was a victory with nationwide significance for antinuclear groups.

From Creek Road the ride proceeds up Sound Road to the village of Wading River, which dates from earliest colonial times. The village prospered as a small farming center for most of its history, but perhaps because of its somewhat remote location, it never grew to any appreciable size. Except for the auto traffic and the few small new buildings at its center, it probably looks much as it did in its earliest days. At the western edge of the village at North Country and Gabriel Mills roads is the Wading River Historical Society headquarters, a restored early-nineteenth-century house. Farther east on North Wading River Road is the Wading River Congregational Church, built around 1830, replacing the original meeting house built in 1740. At the intersection of North Wading River Road and North Country Road is the Miller Homestead, a brown weathered structure built in 1797.

We proceed south from Wading River on North Country Road to Sound Avenue and the beginning of a 6-mile run through pleasant rolling farmland. It comes as a surprise to most people to learn that Suffolk County, usually thought of as part of the New York megalopolis, is a leading agricultural county in New York State. A recent U.S. Agricultural Census indicates that Suffolk County was first in the state in agricultural income, flower growing, number of nurseries, acreage of sod, potato production, output of ducks, number of acres irrigated, and number of large farms. It was second in the growth of strawberries. The local produce can be sampled at the farm stands along Sound Avenue.

At the end of Edwards Avenue we head back toward Wildwood Park on Route 25. There is usually some traffic here, but the road has a wide shoulder. We turn north on Hulse Landing Road back to the park. Wildwood Park offers a pleasant beach, refreshments and rest rooms, and roads and paths from which cyclists can observe the good life in outdoor and vehicle camping.

Riverhead

Number of miles:	20
Approximate pedaling time:	4 hours
Terrain:	Flat with some hilly stretches on the north shore
Surface:	Good; some sandy sections
Traffic:	Heavy in Riverhead, light to moderate elsewhere
Things to see:	Suffolk County Government Center, Pier Avenue Beach, Sound Avenue, Jamesport Town Beach, Suffolk County Historical Society Museum

This is a long but easy ride through the varied neighborhoods of the town of Riverhead. The area is the most heavily urbanized in eastern Long Island, containing a mix of industrial and commercial activity and farming. As in most places on Long Island, the sea is not far away—in addition to its developed sections, Riverhead has its share of attractive beachfronts on Long Island Sound and Great Peconic Bay.

The ride starts from Riverhead on the Peconic River. The original English settlers appeared here in 1690, after which the village grew slowly into a major commercial center, capitalizing on its strategic location at the head of Peconic Bay. About ½ mile west of the ride starting point, on the south side of the river, is the Suffolk County Government Center, an imposing display of governmental architecture.

We progress north on the Northville Turnpike along a stretch of bland residential buildings and flat scrubland. About 2 miles out, however, we begin to get a view of the more hilly and attractive farmlands of the north section of the area. After crossing Route 105, a four-lane speedway connecting Long Island's north and south forks,

55

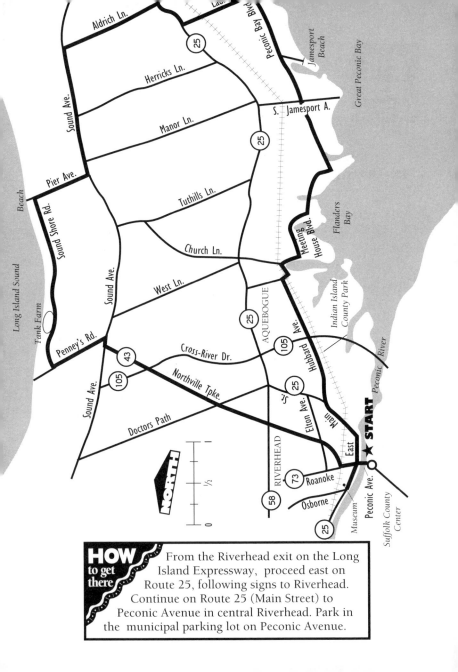

Aldrich Ln.

Peconic Bay Blvd.

Lad...

25

Jamesport Beach

Great Peconic Bay

Herricks Ln.

Sound Ave.

S. Jamesport A.

Manor Ln.

25

Pier Ave.

Beach

Sound Shore Rd.

Tuthills Ln.

Meeting House Blvd.

Flanders Bay

Long Island Sound

Church Ln.

Sound Ave.

West Ln.

Tank Farm

Penney's Rd.

25

AQUEBOGUE

Indian Island County Park

Cross-River Dr.

43

105

Hubbard Ave.

Peconic River

Sound Ave.

105

Northville Tpke.

25

NORTH

½

0

Doctors Path

25

Main St.

Elton Ave.

East

★ START

RIVERHEAD

73

Roanoke

58

Osborne

Museum

Peconic Ave.

Suffolk County Center

25

HOW to get there

From the Riverhead exit on the Long Island Expressway, proceed east on Route 25, following signs to Riverhead. Continue on Route 25 (Main Street) to Peconic Avenue in central Riverhead. Park in the municipal parking lot on Peconic Avenue.

DIREC-TIONS at a glance

- Start from the municipal parking lot on Peconic Avenue in Riverhead.
- Right onto Peconic Avenue from the parking lot to East Main Street (Route 25).
- Jog right on East Main to the first left, Roanoke Avenue (County Road 73).
- Left on Roanoke four blocks to Northville Turnpike (County Road 43) just past the railroad tracks.
- Right on Northville Turnpike about 3½ miles to Sound Avenue, crossing County Road 58 and Route 105.
- Jog right on Sound Avenue to Penney's Road on the left.
- Left on Penney's Road about ½ mile to its end at Sound Shore Road.
- Right on Sound Shore Road past the tank farm, about 2½ miles to its end at Pier Avenue.
- Left on Pier Avenue to the beach on Long Island Sound.
- Return on Pier Avenue about ½ mile to Sound Avenue.
- Left on Sound Avenue about 1½ miles to Aldrich Lane.
- Right on Aldrich Lane about 1½ miles to Route 25 (going right at Franklinville Road).
- Right on Route 25 about ¼ mile to Laurel Lane on the left.
- Left on Laurel Lane about ¾ mile to Peconic Bay Boulevard.
- Right on Peconic Bay Boulevard about 4½ miles to its end at Meeting House Creek Boulevard.
- Right on Meeting House Creek Boulevard to Hubbard Avenue, just past the railroad tracks.
- Left on Hubbard Avenue about 2 miles to East Main Street in Riverhead.
- Left on East Main Street about 1 mile to Peconic Avenue in central Riverhead.
- Left on Peconic Avenue to the ride starting point.

we come to Sound Avenue and Penney's Road.

Continuing north on Penney's Road we come to Sound Shore Road, on which we head east along a heavily wooded crest overlooking beautiful farms south, and, visible through the trees here and there, Long Island Sound to the north. About a mile along we come to a fuel-oil tank farm consisting of a collection of huge oil-storage tanks painted an inconspicuous green. It is apparent that efforts have been made here to minimize the visual blight, but nonetheless it remains an eyesore. The problem extends to the waterside also, where from the beach at the end of Pier Avenue can be seen the offshore loading platform of the tank farm and, at times, the tankers unloading their cargo.

From the beach at Pier Avenue we head south back to Sound Avenue, then east, then south again on Aldrich Lane. This 3-mile leg is the very antithesis of the oil-storage tank farm and of industrialization in general. In sharp contrast to the first part of the ride, we are brought back to a different age and lifestyle in the rich, quiet, green, and bountiful farms of the area. Descriptions of Sound Avenue dating from the 1800s portray a scene much like that seen today along this unique road. It remains one of the most attractive country roads in the New York City vicinity.

At the end of this segment we go south on Laurel Lane to the shore of the north fork on Great Peconic Bay. We head west on Peconic Bay Boulevard, with farmland to the north and vacation homes on pleasant narrow lanes running to the bay to the south. About 1½ miles along we come to the Jamesport Town Beach at which you can swim and obtain refreshments if you wish. It offers an excellent view of the bay, across which the Shinnecock Hills of the south fork can be seen. The pleasant scenery of Peconic Bay Boulevard continues for about 3 miles to the village of Aquebogue. From here we continue for about 2 miles, paralleling the railroad tracks along Hubbard Avenue back into Riverhead on East Main Street.

Main Street, of course, offers many eating places and the opportunity to browse around a busy downtown shopping area. For something quieter you might try the Suffolk County Historical Society Museum about two blocks west on Main Street at Osborn Avenue. It displays interesting artifacts of three centuries of Suffolk County history.

Mattituck—Cutchogue

Number of miles:	15
Approximate pedaling time:	3 hours
Terrain:	Flat
Surface:	Good; sandy in places
Traffic:	Light except for Route 25, which can have heavy traffic
Things to see:	Octagonal Building, Mattituck Inlet, Cutchogue Village Green museum complex, New Suffolk village, Mattituck Airport

Mattituck and Cutchogue are two of the oldest communities in the town of Southold, both dating from around 1650. They are located on sites of former Indian villages, Cutchogue being named after a tribe that controlled most of the land in the area. Mattituck Inlet, at the head of which sits Mattituck Village, runs 2 miles into the north fork from Long Island Sound and is the only harbor on the 50-mile or so stretch between Port Jefferson and Orient Point. Cutchogue faces Little Peconic Bay to the south. Both villages were farming centers, collecting the produce of the productive farms that surround them. Mattituck especially was known for its fruits and vegetables, particularly its great quantities of strawberries. During the last ten years it has also become a center of grape growing and wine making—new agricultural activities for Long Island. Although the farming character of the land remains, it is fast being changed as more and more vacationing people travel through the area and as the land is converted from farming to residential use.

The ride starts from Mattituck where at the intersection of Love Lane and Route 25, on the left, is an octagonal building, an architectural shape quite popular on Long Island in the 1800s. We turn right

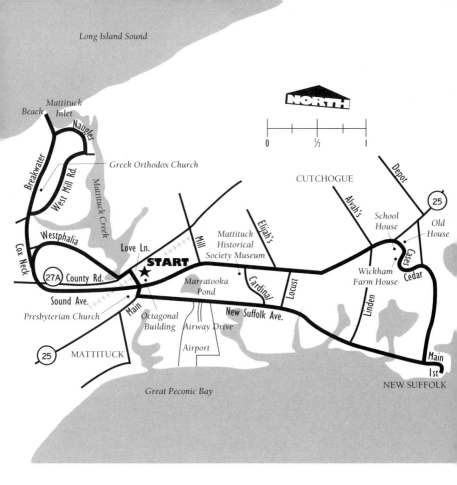

Long Island Sound

Mattituck Beach

Mattituck Inlet

Naugles

Breakwater

West Mill Rd.

Greek Orthodox Church

Mattituck Creek

Westphalia

Cox Neck

27A County Rd.

Love Ln.

START

Mill

Mattituck Historical Society Museum

Elijah's

CUTCHOGUE

Alvah's

Depot

25

School House

Old House

Cases

Wickham Farm House

Cedar

Sound Ave.

Presbyterian Church

Main

Octagonal Building

Marratooka Pond

Airway Drive

Cardinal

Locust

New Suffolk Ave.

Linden

25

MATTITUCK

Airport

Main

1st

Great Peconic Bay

NEW SUFFOLK

NORTH

0   ½   1

HOW to get there
East 10 miles from the end of the Long Island Expressway at Riverhead on Route 25, through Aquebogue, Jamesport, and Laurel to Mattituck. Left on Love Lane, off Route 25 just past the Mattituck Presbyterian Church. Park in the railroad parking lot one block north of Route 25.

- From Love Lane, Mattituck, proceed south to the Route 25 intersection and then right on Sound Avenue. The octagonal building is on the left.
- Continue for 1 mile on Sound Avenue to County Route 48 (also known as County Road 27 and Route 27A).
- Cross County Route 48 and proceed on Cox Neck Road for about ¾ mile to Breakwater Road (Luthers Road farther on) on the left.
- Left on Breakwater Road about 1¼ miles to its end at Mattituck Inlet.
- Return to Naugles Drive, the first road on the left.
- Left on Naugles Drive about ½ mile to its end at West Mill Road.
- Right on West Mill Road about 1 mile, continuing on to Cox Neck Road.
- Continue on Cox Neck Road about ¼ mile to Westphalia Road on the left.
- Left on Westphalia Road about ¼ mile to County Route 48.
- Left on County Route 48 to Love Lane.
- Right on Love Lane past the ride starting point to Route 25.
- Left on Route 25 about 2¾ miles to Cases Lane in Cutchogue. Along the way on the right, near Cardinal Drive, is the Mattituck Historical Society Museum.
- Right on Cases Lane past the Old House, Old Schoolhouse, and the Wickham Farmhouse, to its end at Cedar Road.
- Left on Cedar Road through the Cedar Golf Club to New Suffolk Road.
- Right on New Suffolk Road 1¼ miles to Main Street, New Suffolk.
- Left on Main Street to First Street, then right to the beach and return.
- Continue west on Main Street, then New Suffolk Avenue, 3 miles back to main road, Route 25, Mattituck, passing Mattituck Airport at Airway Drive on the left opposite Marratooka Pond.
- Right on Route 25 at Mattituck Presbyterian Church to the ride starting point on Love Lane.

here and head west on Sound Avenue, over the railroad tracks and, farther on, County Route 48 onto Cox Neck Road. This is a quiet rural road that passes through farmland and patches of scrub oak. Farther on, on Breakwater Road, is the open farmland that once covered the entire area. Coming in on the left are the roads of communities of homes built in the 1950s.

At the end of Breakwater Road we come to Mattituck Inlet on Long Island Sound. The inlet itself consists of parallel rock jetties, 150 feet apart, forming a channel for the swift-moving inlet stream. Directly behind the beach can be seen vacation homes that are very much in demand because of their view of Long Island Sound and the relatively short travel time to New York City.

We return to Mattituck through pleasant farm country on Mill Road and proceed onto Westphalia Road, an older residential area bordering Mattituck Creek. At the intersection of Westphalia and County Route 48 is a good view of the head of Mattituck Creek and one of its quiet arms, comfortably harboring sailboats, outboards, and other small craft.

From Mattituck we head east toward Cutchogue on heavily trafficked Route 25. On the right, about a mile along at Cardinal Drive, is the Mattituck Historical Society Museum. The building is a restored house built originally around 1800. In Cutchogue we turn right on Cases Lane and come to a cluster of historic buildings on the Cutchogue Village Green. On the left is the Old House, built in 1649, and on the right, the old Schoolhouse Museum, built around 1850. Also on the right is the William Wickham House, an early American home built in the 1740s. The buildings are worth seeing for their collections of colonial and postcolonial furnishings and artifacts.

We proceed south from the Village Green to New Suffolk on Little Peconic Bay. This community dates from the mid-1800s when its beautiful bayside location was first developed as a summer vacation area. From the beach at the end of First Street is a view of Robbins Island to the south and Little Hog Neck and Nassau Point to the east. A sign on Main Street notes that this was the location of the Holland Submarine Company, which was in business for a while here at the turn of the century.

We return to Mattituck on New Suffolk Road with Great Peconic Bay on the left. This road crosses extremely attractive tidelands and passes a number of beautiful homes along the bay. Just before reaching Mattituck we pass Marratooka Pond on the right, around which are several attractive homes. On the left, at Airway Drive, is the entrance to Mattituck Airport, where small private aircraft can be perused close up. At Route 25 is historic Mattituck Presbyterian Church, an imposing colonial structure, and beyond that the ride starting point at Love Lane.

Southold—Bayview

Number of miles:	14
Approximate pedaling time:	3 hours
Terrain:	Moderately hilly
Surface:	Good; sandy in places
Traffic:	Heavy in Southold, light elsewhere
Things to see:	Southold Burying Ground, Custer Institute, Horton Point Town Park and Museum, Hashamomuck Beach, Thomas Moore House

Southold shares with Southampton the distinction of being the oldest English settlement on Long Island. Settlers first arrived in 1640, having encamped first in New Haven, across Long Island Sound in Connecticut. Their names—Youngs, Horton, Ackerly, Wells, Corey—are echoed in the names of the streets and avenues of the present village of Southold and the peninsula of Bayview. They were hard workers and staunch Puritans, for many years allowing only members of the church to share in the civil authority of the community. The discipline and fortitude of the founders and their descendants caused Southold to become early on one of the most successful farming communities on Long Island. The town of Southold is still a prosperous farm area, and the village of Southold at its center exhibits a small-town coziness only partly offset by the heavy traffic of summer visitors.

The ride proceeds from the village of Southold south through Bayview, or Great Hog Neck, to Southold Bay and Little Peconic Bay, then north back through Southold to Horton Point on Long Island Sound, then back to Southold. It provides a good mixture of farming and nautical environments, blended with a comfortable historical ambience.

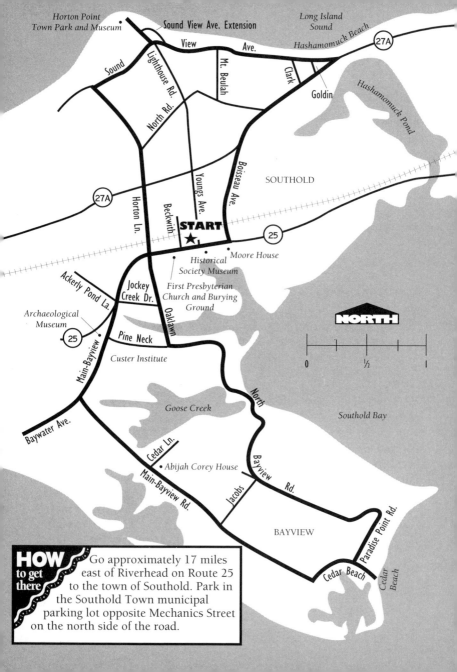

Horton Point
Town Park and Museum

Sound View Ave. Extension

Long Island
Sound

Hashamomuck Beach

27A

Sound

View

Ave.

Hashamomuck

Mt. Beulah

Clark

Goldin

Hashamomuck Pond

Lighthouse Rd.

North Rd.

Boisseau Ave.

SOUTHOLD

27A

Horton Ln.

Beckwith

Youngs Ave.

START
★

25

Moore House

Historical
Society Museum

First Presbyterian
Church and Burying
Ground

Ackerly Pond La.

Jockey
Creek Dr.

Oaklawn

Archaeological
Museum

25

Pine Neck

Main-Bayview

Custer Institute

NORTH

0   ½   1

Goose Creek

North

Southold Bay

Baywater Ave.

Cedar Ln.

• Abijah Corey House

Main-Bayview Rd.

Jacobs

Bayview   Rd.

BAYVIEW

Paradise Point Rd.

Cedar Beach

Cedar
Beach

HOW
to get
there

Go approximately 17 miles
east of Riverhead on Route 25
to the town of Southold. Park in
the Southold Town municipal
parking lot opposite Mechanics Street
on the north side of the road.

DIREC-TIONS at a glance

- Start from the municipal parking lot opposite Mechanics Street on Route 25, Southold. Proceed out onto Route 25 (Main Street) and right (west) for about 1 mile past the First Presbyterian Church on the left to Bayview Road on the left fork, just past Jockey Creek Drive on the left and Ackerly Pond Lane on the right.
- Follow Bayview Road for about 3 miles to its end at Cedar Beach Road, passing the Archaeological Museum and Custer Institute, and farther on at Cedar Lane, the Abijah Corey House.
- Left on Cedar Beach Road about ½ mile to Cedar Beach.
- Returning from Cedar Beach, take the first right onto Paradise Point Road for about ½ mile to North Bayview Road.
- Left on North Bayview Road for about 1 mile to Jacobs Lane on the left. Go right here, continuing on North Bayview Road for about 1¾ miles, over the Goose Creek Bridge, to its end at Pine Neck Road.
- Left on Pine Neck Road about ½ mile to Oaklawn Avenue on right.
- Right on Oaklawn Avenue, over the bridge, to its end at Route 25 (Main Street).
- Jog right on Route 25; then turn left onto Horton Lane.
- Continue on Horton Lane, across Route 27A, about 1½ miles to Soundview Avenue.
- Right on Soundview Avenue to Lighthouse Road.
- Left on Lighthouse Road to Horton Point Town Park and Museum.
- From Horton Point return on the first left, Soundview Avenue Extension, to Soundview Avenue.
- Continue left on Soundview Avenue for about 1½ miles to the intersection with Route 27A near Hashamomuck Beach.
- From the beach go right (west) on 27A about 1¼ miles to Boisseau Avenue and the turnoff to Southold.
- Follow the Southold sign left onto Boisseau Avenue and continue for ¾ mile over the railroad tracks to Route 25, Southold.
- Right on Route 25 past the Thomas Moore House and the Southold Historical Society Museum to the municipal parking lot.

Proceeding west on Main Street (Route 25), we pass on the left the First Presbyterian Church of Southold and the Southold Burying Ground. The church building was erected in 1803, but predecessors date from 1640 when it was organized as the First Church Congregation of Southold. A marker notes that the church burying ground is the oldest English burying ground in New York State. As we continue onto Bayview Road we come to the New York State Archaeological Society Museum, which displays Long Island Indian artifacts, pottery, and sculpture. Directly opposite it is the Custer Institute with its domed observatory. The institute is the home of a private astronomy study group that maintains the observatory and its equipment. It's open to the public at various times during the summer.

Farther south on Main-Bayview Road, just north of Cedar Lane, is the Abijah Corey House, built in the early 1700s. It shows its age and contrasts sharply with the modern homes that surround it. As we continue on Main-Bayview Road we turn left at the General Wayne Inn, an excellent restaurant, and come to Cedar Beach at the end of Cedar Beach Road. This is a quarter-mile pebbly beach on Little Peconic Bay providing no amenities but offering unsupervised swimming and a good view of the bay. Just back of the beach is a concrete structure housing the Suffolk County Community College Marine Science Center. From here we continue on North Bayview Road and leave Bayview on the Goose Creek Bridge. There is a great view of Southold Bay to the east and Goose Creek, a pleasant tranquil backwater, to the west.

We proceed back through Southold and then north on Horton Lane, a sparsely developed area of farms and flat woodlands, onto Sound View Avenue and Lighthouse Road to Horton Point Town Park and Museum. The lighthouse at the park dates from 1857. At the end of Lighthouse Road is a stair leading to the beach on Long Island Sound. Stairs of this type, common all along the the north shore, often require rebuilding as erosion eats the soft bluffs away. From the top of the stair is an unobstructed view of Connecticut on the horizon.

Going east on Sound View Avenue, on rather hilly terrain, we pass through a heavily treed stretch (which unfortunately blocks the Sound view) and come to Hashamomuck Beach on Long Island

Sound. This is a long, wide beach providing swimming, refreshments, and rest rooms. It is flanked by hotels and motels and is usually frequented by a good-sized crowd. We return to Southold on Boisseau Avenue and come to the Thomas Moore House on the south side of Route 25. This structure was built prior to 1658 and has recently been restored. Farther on, at Maple Lane, is the Southold Historical Society Museum, a cluster of four buildings displaying antique home decorations, toys, tools, carriages, and other items.

Greenport—Orient Point

Number of miles:	21
Approximate pedaling time:	4 hours
Terrain:	Flat
Surface:	Good; sandy in places
Traffic:	Heavy in Greenport, light to moderate elsewhere
Things to see:	East Marion Orient Park beach, Orient Point ferry landing, Orient Village, Greenport

This ride explores the eastern tip of Long Island's north fork from Greenport to Orient Point. It runs on a narrow peninsula never more than 1½ miles wide. At points, only a few hundred feet of sandy soil separate Long Island Sound on the north from Orient Harbor on the south. This ride provides the most striking example of the mingled farm and sea environments of eastern Long Island. At times the feel and tang of the sea predominate, but this can change suddenly to an air of earthy farmland as one passes by fertile and ripe fields. It is an experience that is available to cyclists in few other places and makes this a most pleasant ride.

The ride starts from the Long Island Railroad parking lot adjacent to the Shelter Island ferry slip in Greenport. Proceeding east we go past the Island's End Golf and Country Club through East Marion and continue on about 2 miles to the narrowest section of the peninsula, with Orient Harbor on the right and tranquil Dam Pond on the left. Orient Harbor presents an attractive waterscape, with the tip of Orient Beach State Park straight ahead and the village of Orient to the left. A half mile farther on is the East Marion Orient Park, with its long stretches of inviting Long Island Sound beach.

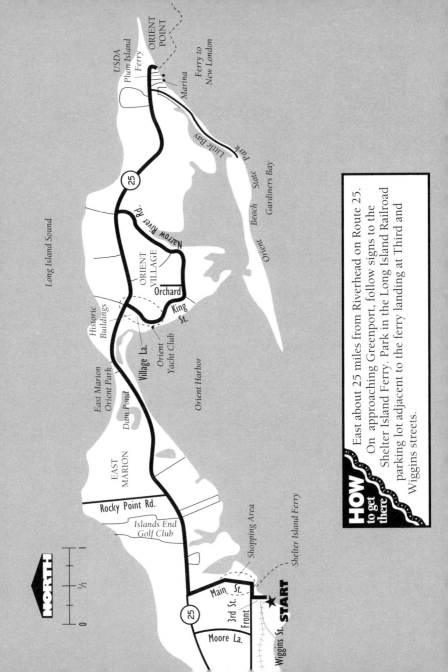

NORTH

Long Island Sound

ORIENT POINT

USDA
Plum Island Ferry

Marina

Ferry to New London

Little Bay

Beach State Park

Gardiners Bay

Orient

25

Narrow River Rd.

ORIENT VILLAGE

Orchard

King St.

Village La.

Orient Yacht Club

Historic Buildings

East Marion Orient Park

Dam Pond

Orient Harbor

EAST MARION

Rocky Point Rd.

Islands End Golf Club

Shopping Area

Shelter Island Ferry

Main St.

3rd St.

Front

★ START

Wiggins St.

Moore La.

25

0   ½   1

HOW to get there

East about 25 miles from Riverhead on Route 25. On approaching Greenport, follow signs to the Shelter Island Ferry. Park in the Long Island Railroad parking lot adjacent to the ferry landing at Third and Wiggins streets.

DIREC-TIONS at a glance

- Start from the railroad station parking lot at Wiggins and Third streets, Greenport.
- Proceed onto Third Street and then up one block to Front Street.
- Right on Front Street to its end at Main Street.
- Left on Main Street, following signs to 25 East, about ¾ mile to Route 25 (Main Road).
- Right (east) on Route 25 on the designated bikeway shoulder for about 8 miles to its end at the Orient Point Ferry. East Marion Orient Park Beach is on the left, halfway along.
- Return on Route 25 for about 2½ miles to Narrow River Road on the left.
- Left on Narrow River Road for about 2 miles, bearing left at the Narrow River Mariner, halfway along, to its end at King Street.
- Right on King Street about 1 mile to Village Lane.
- Right on Village Lane through Orient Village Historic District, for about 1 mile, to its end at Route 25.
- Left (west) on Route 25 for about 5 miles to Main Street, Greenport.
- Left on Main Street through the Greenport shopping area, to its end at Front Street.
- Right on Front Street to Third Street.
- Left on Third Street to Wiggins Street and the ride starting point at the railroad parking lot.

We continue on Route 25 on a wide, smooth shoulder lane all the way to the end of the north fork. This entire stretch is becoming more heavily developed and trafficked on the Long Island Sound side as vacation homes and condominiums rise along the water's edge. At the end of Route 25 we find the Orient Point Ferry to New London, Connecticut, and just west of it is a modern private marina where meals and snacks are served. The ferries come almost to the beach in a narrow, crude slip where they discharge vehicles and passengers through clam-shell openings at their bows.

Also at Orient Point is the departure point for the United States Department of Agriculture Plum Island facility. Plum Island, 2 miles out in Long Island Sound, is the site of extensive investigation of animal diseases, many of which are highly contagious. Great care is taken to control all contact with the labs, hence the tall fences around the docks. A quarter mile west of here is the entrance to the Orient Beach State Park. There is a narrow road that runs for about 2 miles to the park beach, providing a great view of Gardiners Bay to the south and narrow Little Bay to the north, the latter filled with marsh grass teeming with seabirds.

We return toward Greenport on Route 25, turning off at Narrow River Road into the village of Orient. This community dates from the mid-1600s when the earliest Southold settlers arrived. The village contains a number of interesting historic structures, including the Shaw House (c. 1730), the Orient Point School House (c. 1888), the Oysterponds Historical Society Museum (four buildings c. 1790 to 1890), the Orient Methodist Church (c. 1835), and the Webb House Museum (c. 1740). All of these are clustered on Village Road. Orient has maintained its small-town coziness and is a most pleasant place for a stop.

We continue west from Orient on Route 25, turning south at the sign for Greenport. The railroad reached Greenport in 1844, at which time the town was just beginning to grow. The village supported a small whaling fleet and several menhaden fish-processing plants—evil-smelling operations that provided fish oil and fertilizers. Hopes that a major link with New England would be formed with the railroad and ferry service never quite panned out, and the village grew slowly to its present size.

The Greenport shopping area, specifically Front and Main streets, is worth visiting. It contains a number of boutiques, bookshops, and art galleries. At the foot of Main Street is Preston's, a ship chandlery that offers every conceivable type of marine hardware, clothing, and equipment, and a large selection of books, ship models, and nautical paintings. Farther north on Main, between Adams and South streets, is the Sterling Historical Society of Greenport Museum.

Five Towns—Long Beach

Number of miles:	20
Approximate pedaling time:	4 hours
Terrain:	Flat
Surface:	Good
Traffic:	Medium to heavy
Things to see:	Old Gristmill Museum, Woodmere Town Dock, Rock Hall, Atlantic Beach and Long Beach boardwalks

This ride encircles the inlet-strewn bays between the Five Towns area bordering New York City, Atlantic Beach, and Island Park, Oceanside, and East Rockaway in southern Nassau County. There is great variation in lifestyles to observe among these communities and several interesting stops along the way.

The ride begins from Lister Park at Ocean Avenue in Rockville Center. It proceeds through the park into East Rockaway, a typical older Long Island suburban area of comfortable appearance. At the intersection of Denton and Woods avenues we come to the Old Gristmill Museum, a weathered gray building dating from 1688, since restored, that once stood on the Mill River, probably close to where Lister Park is now. It displays nineteenth-century Long Island village life and work scenes, as well as tools and implements used at the time.

About 1¾ miles farther on, at Deering Lane and Main Street, begin about 6 miles of curving quiet roads bordered by large and attractive homes. This is the southern section of the Five Towns area—Hewlett, Woodmere, Cedarhurst, Inwood, and Lawrence—one of the earliest settled areas on Long Island. It is situated at the head of a peninsula that reaches down and around Jamaica Bay to the west. At one time Five Towns was heavily farmed, but with the coming of the railroad

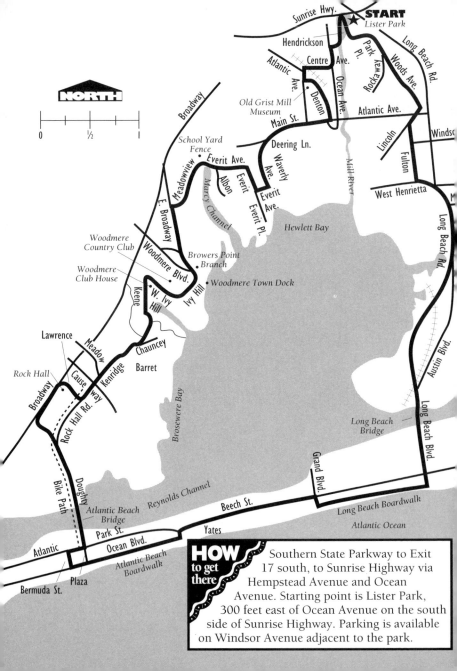

- Start at Lister Park, Rockville Center.
- Proceed through Lister Park along the Mill River to the park exit at South Park Avenue.
- Right on South Park Avenue to Ocean Avenue.
- Left on Ocean Avenue ¼ mile to Centre Avenue.
- Right on Centre Avenue, over railroad tracks, to Atlantic Avenue.
- Left on Atlantic Avenue to Woods Avenue.
- Left on Woods Avenue to Denton Avenue.
- Continue on Denton Avenue to Atlantic Avenue.
- Right on Atlantic Avenue ¼ mile to merge with Main Street; continue on Main ¾ mile to Deering Lane on the left.
- Left on Deering Lane around to Waverly Avenue.
- Left on Waverly to Everit Avenue on the right.
- Right on Everit Avenue to Everit Place.
- Right at Everit Place, continuing on Everit Avenue (the road turns, but it is still Everit Avenue) to Albon Road.
- Right at Albon Road, continuing on Everit, around Marcy Channel to Meadowview Avenue at the schoolground fence.
- Left on Meadowview Avenue about ¾ mile to East Broadway.
- Left on East Broadway to its end at Browers Point Branch (not Brower Avenue).
- Left on Browers Point Branch to Woodmere Boulevard; left on Woodmere Boulevard to its end at the Woodmere Town Dock.
- Out of the town dock back up Woodmere Boulevard to Ivy Hill Road on the left.
- Left on Ivy Hill Road, which becomes West Ivy Hill Road, bordering the Woodmere Club grounds to Keene Lane.
- Left on Keene Lane through the Woodmere Club grounds to Atlantic Avenue.
- Right on Atlantic Avenue approximately ¼ mile to the merge with Chauncey Lane on the left.
- Continue right on Chauncey Lane to the intersection with Auerbach Lane, Barret Road, Cedarhurst Avenue, and Briarwood X.
- Left at the intersection onto Barret Road to Washington Avenue on the right.

- Right on Washington Avenue to Kenridge Avenue.
- Left on Kenridge Avenue to merge with Meadow Lane.
- Continue left on Meadow, across Causeway Road, onto Rock Hall Road.
- Continue on Rock Hall Road to Lawrence Avenue.
- Right on Lawrence Avenue to Broadway. Rock Hall is on the left at the intersection.
- Left on Broadway ½ mile to Doughty Boulevard.
- Left on Doughty Boulevard, 1 mile, to the Atlantic Beach Bridge.
- Over the bridge to Atlantic Boulevard.
- Jog right on Atlantic Boulevard to Bermuda Street.
- Left on Bermuda Street to Ocean Boulevard.
- Left on Ocean Boulevard approximately 1¼ miles to its end at Yates Avenue.
- Left on Yates one block to Park Street.
- Right on Park Street (Beech Street farther on) 1¾ miles to Grand Boulevard.
- Right on Grand Boulevard to the Long Beach Boardwalk.
- Left on the boardwalk 1¼ miles to Long Beach Boulevard exit ramp.
- Off the boardwalk onto Long Beach Boulevard, then over the Long Beach Bridge, to Bridge Plaza.
- At Bridge Plaza follow the Island Park signs, continuing on Long Beach Boulevard to the left.
- Through Island Park and Barnum Island on Long Beach Road, approximately 1¾ miles, over the railroad tracks, to the intersection with Austin Boulevard.
- Continue on Long Beach Road to the left at Austin Boulevard intersection for approximately 1¼ miles to West Henrietta Avenue in Oceanside.
- Left on Henrietta to Fulton Avenue.
- Right on Fulton Avenue ¾ mile to merge with Lincoln Avenue on the left.
- Continue right on Lincoln, across Atlantic Avenue to Woods Avenue on the left.
- Left on Woods Avenue 1 mile to the merge with Rockaway Avenue on the left.

- Continue across Rockaway Avenue onto Park Place.
- Continue on Park Place to South Park Avenue.
- Left on South Park Avenue to Hendrickson Avenue.
- Right on Hendrickson Avenue to the Lister Park entrance, then through the park back to the ride starting point.

---

in the early 1800s it became a center for vacationers heading for the Rockaways farther out on the peninsula. It is now a commuters' colony whose proximity to New York City and the bays and waterfront of the Long Island south shore make it a most desirable place to live (despite the screaming jets going into and out of Kennedy International Airport, 3 miles to the west).

Halfway along this leg, at the end on Woodmere Boulevard in Hewlett Neck, is the Woodmere Town Dock, a good resting spot providing an excellent view of Brosewere Bay and the marshy islands that are typical of the Nassau County south shore. The ride continues from here along the Woodmere Club to Keene Lane, where we cut through the Woodmere Club grounds and go through a marshy area at the head of Woodmere Channel Basin. In the early morning hours this area is alive with shorebirds of all kinds.

Farther on in Lawrence, we come to Rock Hall, one of the most celebrated colonial homes on Long Island. It is an imposing Georgian-style building built in the late 1700s for Josiah Martin, a wealthy West Indies planter. It is furnished with eighteenth-century antiques that accurately re-create home decorations for this type of house when it was in active use.

From Rock Hall we proceed south over Reynolds Channel on the Atlantic Beach Bridge to the community of Atlantic Beach. Atlantic Beach, and Long Beach just east of it, extend for 5½ miles on the first of the barrier beaches that border the entire south shore of Long Island. These towns were developed in the late nineteenth century as vacation and recreation areas. They are now primarily year-round residential communities, although there is still a considerable summer inflow of vacationers. The Atlantic Beach and Long Beach boardwalks are most enjoyable. From here you get an open ocean view, the opportunity for a swim, and access to a number of snack shops and restaurants.

From Long Beach we go back over Reynolds Channel on the Long Beach Bridge for the 6½-mile return leg to Lister Park. Just over the bridge we traverse Island Park, home of U.S. Senator Alfonse D'Amato, and then proceed through Oceanside. These communities are much like East Rockaway at the beginning of the ride.

Great River—Oakdale

Number of miles:	Great River—9; Oakdale—4
Approximate pedaling time:	Great River—2 hours; Oakdale—1 hour
Terrain:	Flat
Surface:	Good; sandy in places
Traffic:	Light
Things to see:	Connetquot River, Timber Point Park, Heckscher State Park, Bayard Cutting Arboretum, Dowling College, Artists' Colony Historic District

The ride consists of two separate segments: the first through Great River on the west bank of the Connetquot, the second through the Idle Hour section of Oakdale on the east bank. Although it is possible to cover the entire course continuously, doing so would require cycling on an extremely dangerous length of Montauk Highway at the head of the river. It is recommended, therefore, that first Great River, then Oakdale be cycled, with the trip between the starting points done by automobile.

The Great River segment begins from the river access road near Timber Point Park. Immediately ahead is the Connetquot River flowing gently to Nicoll Bay. The Connetquot meanders south from the middle of Long Island, starting as a small stream but eventually widening into one of the largest and most attractive rivers on the island. Directly south is the Timber Point County Park, where we see a handsome columned clubhouse surrounded by neatly clipped and tended fairways and greens. You can ride down to the west and east marinas in the park for a close-up view of some of the beautiful craft that ply the river. From the rear of the clubhouse is an expansive view over the course and the bay.

HOW to get there

Exit 45 East on Heckscher State Parkway, east one block on South Country Road (Route 27A) to Great River Road. South on Great River Road about 1½ miles to the river access road on the left near Timber Point Park.

Sunrise Hwy.

27

27

Heckscher

Bayard Cutting Arboretum

Dowling College

★ START
Oakdale

Oakdale
RR Station

Exit 45

Montauk

Hwy.

27A

27A

Idle Hour Blvd.

Shore Dr.

Hollywood Dr.

Middlesex

Jade La.

Artist Colony

Vanderbilt Blvd.

Overlook

Shore Dr.

Great River Rd.

Country Village Ln.

State

Timber Pt. Rd.

Parkway

Boat Yard

Connetquot River

★ START
Great River

River Rd.

Pedestrian Entrance

Timber Point

County Park

Heckscher State Park

Nicoll Bay

Beach

Great South Bay

NORTH

0   ½   1

- Park on the side street running to the Connetquot River just north of Timber Point County Park.
- Proceed into and around the park and return to River Road.
- Left on River Road for about ½ mile to the merge with Timber Point Road.
- Continue on Timber Point Road to the Heckscher State Park pedestrian and bicycle entrance on the left, just past Heckscher Parkway.
- Proceed onto and around the park back to the Timber Point Road entrance.
- Left on Timber Point Road about ¼ mile to Country Village Lane.
- Right on Country Village Lane about ½ mile to its end at Overlook Drive.
- Left on Overlook Drive about ½ mile to Route 27A.
- Right at 27A, following a pedestrian walk under the Parkway overpass, then on for about ½ mile to the Bayard Cutting Arboretum.
- Return on 27A from the arboretum to Great River Road.
- Left on Great River Road about 1½ miles to the ride starting point.
- For the Oakdale segment, drive east on 27A past the merge with Route 27, and on ¼ mile or so past the railroad tracks to Idle Hour Boulevard. Parking is usually available in the store parking areas on Montauk Highway.
- Go south on Idle Hour Boulevard through Dowling College on the right, about ½ mile to Shore Drive.
- Left on Shore Drive to Hollywood Drive.
- Right on Hollywood Drive, continuing right at Jade Street past the Artists' Colony barn to Idle Hour Boulevard at Tower Mews.
- Right on Idle Hour Boulevard to Middlesex Avenue.
- Left on Middlesex Avenue with a short jog right at Grassmen Avenue to Shore Drive.
- Left on Shore Drive for about 1¾ miles to its end at Vanderbilt Boulevard.
- Left on Vanderbilt Boulevard about 1¼ miles to Montauk Highway, then left to the ride starting point.

From Timber Point Park we proceed to Heckscher State Park, one of several major state parks on Long Island. It contains a bicycle path through a couple of miles of wooded picnic areas and playgrounds to a bathing area on Great South Bay. On summer weekends the park is quite crowded, and the cyclist must be wary of pedestrians, especially young children.

From Heckscher Park we go on through a modern housing development to the Bayard Cutting Arboretum. The arboretum is a walkers' park—bicycles must be left at a rack at the entrance. There are five walks in the park, each devoted to a different type of vegetation and wildlife—pine tree, wildflower, rhododendron, swamp cypress, and birds—the latter two bordering on the Connetquot. The arboretum was originally owned by the family of William Bayard Cutting and was later presented as a gift to New York State. From the arboretum we proceed back on Great River Road to the starting point of the Great River Loop.

The second segment of the ride begins at Route 27A near Idle Hour Boulevard in Oakdale. The area is known as Idle Hour from the name of an old estate located here once owned by William Vanderbilt. It's a pleasant little knot of intersecting streets and lanes lined with attractive and comfortable homes. No attempt is made here to map out in detail the maze of streets. Suffice it to say that the community is quite small and that all roads lead back eventually to Shore Drive at its perimeter.

A half mile or so in on Idle Hour Boulevard is Dowling College, the main building of which is the former Vanderbilt mansion. The mansion was built in 1902, and its 110 rooms, extensive stone and woodwork, and palatial appearance have made it a landmark on Long Island. From the stone steps at the rear of the mansion there is an exceptionally attractive view of the Connetquot, and one can easily picture the festive events that once took place here. The building has undergone extensive renovation and repair after a fire damaged a good deal of it in 1973.

If we turn into the maze at Shore Drive we eventually come to the original farm complex purchased by the Vanderbilts, located near Hollywood Drive. The main building is a large old rambling red-brick barn featuring a number of dormers, turrets, and interesting "eyebrow" windows in the roof. This is the centerpiece of the Artists' Colony, a picturesque cluster of dwellings that during the 1920s and 1930s housed a community of artists. The area was declared a Historical District by the town of Islip.

We continue on Shore Drive past the homes lining the river, then over a small bridge overlooking a busy boatyard. Farther on, at Vanderbilt Boulevard, we can reach the water's edge and obtain one last good view before proceeding north to the ride starting point at Montauk Highway.

Smith Point

Number of miles:	9
Approximate pedaling time:	2 hours
Terrain:	Flat
Surface:	Smooth but sandy; one dirt-road section
Traffic:	Light to moderate
Things to see:	Pattersquash Creek, Manor of St. George Museum, Brookhaven Town Beach, Smith Point

This is a pleasant ride that offers the opportunity to see the variety of water views, wetlands, and ocean beaches that abound on the south shore of Long Island. The Mastic peninsula juts into the southern bay, separating the bay into its major sections: Great South Bay to the west and Moriches Bay to the east. Due south from Smith Point, the southern tip of the peninsula, are Fire Island Beach and the open Atlantic.

The peninsula has an interesting colonial past dating from the late seventeenth century, when William Smith of Northampshire, England, at one time governor of Tangiers and later the holder of varied posts in the New York colonial government and militia, purchased from the local Patchogue Indian tribe a large tract of land running from the Connetquot River in the west to the Farge River in the east, and north to the middle of the island. The patent issued for this purchase also included the Strong Neck peninsula just east of the village of Setauket on Long Island's north shore. Mastic was the birthplace of William Floyd, delegate to the first Continental Congress and later one of the signers of the Declaration of Independence, and of Nathaniel Woodhull, who participated in the French and Indian War as a member of the New York colonial army and who later com-

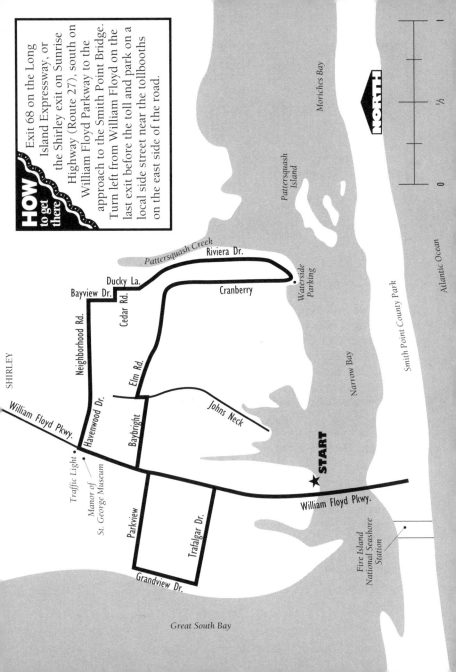

HOW to get there

Exit 68 on the Long Island Expressway, or the Shirley exit on Sunrise Highway (Route 27), south on William Floyd Parkway to the approach to the Smith Point Bridge. Turn left from William Floyd on the last exit before the toll and park on a local side street near the tollbooths on the east side of the road.

NORTH

0   ¼   ½

Moriches Bay

Pattersquash Island

Atlantic Ocean

Smith Point County Park

Narrow Bay

Pattersquash Creek

Riviera Dr.

Ducky La.

Bayview Dr.

Cedar Rd.

Cranberry

Waterside Parking

SHIRLEY

Neighborhood Rd.

Elm Rd.

Johns Neck

Havenwood Dr.

Baybright

William Floyd Pkwy.

Traffic Light

Manor of St. George Museum

★ START

William Floyd Pkwy.

Parkview

Trafalgar Dr.

Fire Island National Seashore Station

Grandview Dr.

Great South Bay

- Start from the parking area near the tollbooths on the east side of William Floyd Parkway.
- Proceed north on William Floyd about 1 mile to Baybright Drive.
- Right on Baybright Drive to Johns Neck Road.
- Jog left on Johns Neck Road to Elm Road on the right.

- Right on Elm Road for about ½ mile to Cranberry Drive.
- Right on Cranberry Drive to its end at the waterside parking area.
- Left on Riviera Drive (unmarked dirt road that Ts into Cranberry Drive near the parking area).
- Continue on Riviera for about 1¼ miles, with Pattersquash Creek on the right, to Ducky Lane.
- Continue on Ducky Lane to Cedar Road.
- Left on Cedar Road to Bayview Drive.
- Right on Bayview Drive, past the merge with Cranberry Drive, to Neighborhood Road.
- Left on Neighborhood Road for about 1 mile to Havenwood Drive on the right.
- Right on Havenwood Drive, over William Floyd Parkway at the traffic light, then left one block on William Floyd Parkway to the Manor of St. George Museum.
- South from the museum on William Floyd about ¼ mile to West Parkview Drive.
- Right on West Parkview Drive to its end at Grand View Drive.
- Left on Grand View Drive to Trafalgar Drive.
- Left on Trafalgar Drive back to William Floyd.
- Right on William Floyd about 1 mile, over the Smith Point Bridge, to Smith Point County Park.
- From Smith Point Park return over the bridge to the ride starting point in the parking area near the tollbooths.

manded a brigade of Suffolk and Queens county militiamen in the American Revolution. A touch of the past remains in the Manor of St. George Museum in the village of Shirley.

The ride starts from the east side of the William Floyd Parkway near the Smith Point Bridge tollbooths and proceeds north on the parkway to Baybright Drive. Although the parkway has wide smooth shoulders, it is sometimes heavily trafficked and should be cycled with care. As we head east on Baybright and Elm and then south on Cranberry Road, we go through typical housing developments that have covered the peninsula since the end of World War II. These contain modestly priced homes on small lots that have provided a haven for young families of moderate income. At the end of Cranberry Road we come to a small parking area on Narrow Bay, the strip of water that separates the peninsula from the barrier beach. To the left is Pattersquash Island, and straight ahead are the dunes of Smith Point County Park. Invariably there is a cool ocean breeze here, which, with the rich surrounding waters, makes it a popular fishing spot. Turning north we follow Riviera Drive along unpaved Pattersquash Creek Road. Pleasant old homes look out on the wetlands, reeds, and waters of the creek, where now and then a small sailboat or outboard goes by.

At the head of Pattersquash Creek we head west back toward William Floyd Parkway, crossing it at Havenwood Drive with the help of a traffic light, and then south a block to the Manor of St. George Museum, a stately, white colonial structure with a striking view of Great South Bay. The estate lands on which this house stands were part of the Smith purchase and were owned by the Smith family until 1954. The museum contains papers and historical documents of the Smith family and its holdings and an outline of Fort St. George, built on the site by the British and destroyed by Americans in 1780.

From the museum we head south on William Floyd Parkway, again on a wide smooth shoulder, then west on Parkview Drive to Grand View Drive. We pass a Brookhaven Town Beach on Great South Bay, where in the late afternoon on clear summer days the bay sparkles under the setting sun.

Rejoining William Floyd Parkway at Trafalgar Drive, we head finally to the ocean beach at Smith Point County Park. There is a short run over the Smith Point Bridge, after which we come immediately to the park parking field and pavilion. Bicycling is not allowed outside the parking areas, but you can lock your bike up in any of the several bike racks and swim in the ocean breakers or just observe them from the dunes to the east and west of the parking fields. Food and refreshments are available at the pavilion. From Smith Point Park it's just a short hop back over the bridge to the ride starting point near the tollbooths.

Westhampton Beach— Quogue

Number of miles:	8½
Approximate pedaling time:	2 hours
Terrain:	Flat
Surface:	Good; sandy in places
Traffic:	Heavy in Westhampton Beach and village center and at points on Dune Road, light to moderate elsewhere
Things to see:	Quogue Schoolhouse Museum, Quogue Presbyterian Church, Phillips Wildlife Refuge

Westhampton Beach and Quogue are the most westerly of the Long Island south shore communities that are strung along the Atlantic beachfront and known collectively as the Hamptons. From here east to Montauk the vacationing is of a special kind, usually associated with substantial wealth and gracious living, but the automobile and road systems available to all have democratized the summer crowd considerably.

Westhampton and Quogue are located on separate peninsulas that divide the south bay between the barrier beach and the island proper into Moriches Bay to the west and Shinnecock Bay to the east. The geography and bridgework are such that a convenient circular bicycle route is available from the villages to the ocean beaches.

The ride starts from Westhampton and proceeds west on Main Street, with its elegant shops and boutiques, to Potunk Lane just past St. Marks Episcopal Church. Across the way is the Westhampton Country Club, discreetly screened from public view. From here we head south toward the ocean through an area of typical Hampton-style homes and vacation retreats. The road is fairly wide, but there is

93

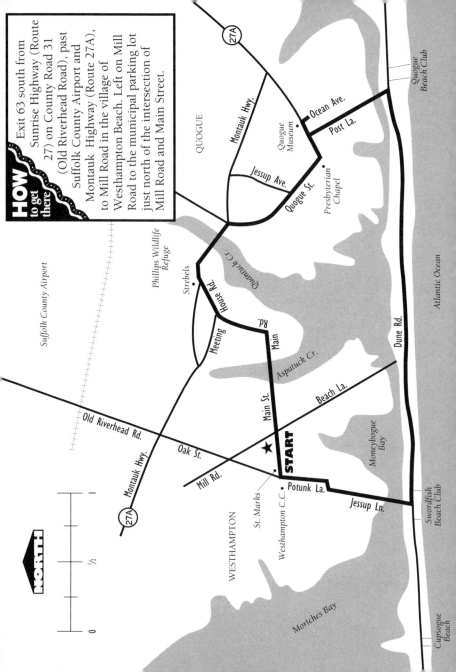

HOW to get there

Exit 63 south from Sunrise Highway (Route 27) on County Road 31 (Old Riverhead Road), past Suffolk County Airport and Montauk Highway (Route 27A), to Mill Road in the village of Westhampton Beach. Left on Mill Road to the municipal parking lot just north of the intersection of Mill Road and Main Street.

NORTH

0   ½   1

27A

Old Riverhead Rd.

Montauk Hwy.

Suffolk County Airport

Phillips Wildlife Refuge

Strebels

Meeting House Rd.

Quantuck C.C.

QUOGUE

27A

Montauk Hwy.

Jessup Ave.

Quogue St.

Ocean Ave.

Post La.

Quogue Museum

Presbyterian Chapel

Quogue Beach Club

Atlantic Ocean

Main Rd.

Main St.

Aspatuck Cr.

Beach La.

Dune Rd.

START

★

Oak St.

Mill Rd.

St. Marks

Westhampton C.C.

Potunk La.

Jessup Ln.

WESTHAMPTON

Moneybogue Bay

Swordfish Beach Club

Moriches Bay

Cupsogue Beach

DIREC-TIONS at a glance

- Start from the municipal parking lot at Mill Road and Main Street.
- Right on Main Street to Potunk Lane. St. Marks Episcopal Church is on the right.
- Left on Potunk Lane past Westhampton Country Club, following signs to the beach for about 1 mile on Potunk Lane, then Jessup Lane.
- Over the bridge from Jessup Lane to Dune Road on Westhampton Beach.
- Left on Dune Road for about 3¼ miles, past Beach Lane Bridge, to Post Lane Bridge in Quogue.
- Over the bridge halfway around the circle onto Post Lane, continuing to its end at Quogue Street.
- Right on Quogue Street to Ocean Avenue and the Quogue Museum and Library.
- Return on Quogue Street from the museum about 1½ miles past the Quogue Presbyterian Chapel at Beach Lane, to Montauk Highway (Route 27A).
- Left on Montauk Highway for about ½ mile, over Quantuck Creek to Meeting House Road, diagonally opposite Strebels Laundry.
- Left on Meeting House Road to Main Road.
- Left on Main Road for about 1 mile, over Aspatuck Creek, to the ride starting point at Mill Road.

some traffic coming and going to the beaches. At the end of Jessup Lane is a bridge to the beach. It has a pedestrian way on which you can leisurely walk your bike over the short span and enjoy the excellent views of Moriches Bay on the right and Moneybogue Bay on the left.

From the end of the bridge we start a 3-mile or so ride along Dune Road, heading for the return bridge at Quogue. You will note immediately the huge beach clubs that line the road in both directions as far as the eye can see. Between the clubs are the homes that have come to symbolize the area—fantastic shapes in wood, featuring angular overhangs, dramatic arcs, circular towers, arches, spans, and every other imaginable architectural device. In the early 1990s, dozens of such homes were damaged or destroyed along the western length of Dune Road during a storm that caused the sea to wash over the roadway.

It's unfortunate that this section of the road has so few public openings to the ocean itself. Almost every foot is spoken for by private homes and clubs. Ocean swimming and viewing are available from Dune Road but at some distance away from Westhampton and Quogue. About a mile west on rebuilt Dune Road is Cupsogue Beach and, to the east, a string of beaches starting at Tiana, about 3 miles from Quogue.

We head north on Post Lane Bridge in Quogue just east of the Quogue Beach Club. Cyclists must be wary here of the often heavy traffic from the eastern beaches. As at Westhampton Beach, the water views from the bridge are excellent. At Quogue Street we turn right to the Quogue Schoolhouse Museum, one block east near Ocean Avenue. It's a weathered building built in 1822, containing artifacts and memorabilia of Quogue and Long Island.

Quogue has been a summer community since the early 1800s, and the homes seem excellently suited to this purpose. They are staid old structures, large and well shaded on spacious groomed lawns, that have about them a quality of substance and comfort. At Beach Lane is the Quogue Presbyterian Chapel, built in 1868, a neat small clapboard structure, and farther on at Jessup Avenue on the right is the village center, consisting of a post office, the village hall, and several real estate offices.

We leave Quogue on Route 27A, heading west back to Westhampton. There is some traffic on this road and it's a bit hilly, but there is a wide smooth shoulder. We pass over Quantuck Creek with its complement of fishermen and to the north observe the tranquil body of water and its surroundings—the Phillips Wildlife Refuge. We turn in from 27A on Meeting House Road, pass over Aspatuck Creek, and arrive back at the ride starting point at Main Street.

Hampton Bays— Shinnecock Canal

Number of miles:	17
Approximate pedaling time:	3 hours
Terrain:	Moderately hilly in Hampton Bays; flat elsewhere
Surface:	Good; sandy in places
Traffic:	Heavy in the village; moderate elsewhere
Things to see:	Shinnecock Canal, Ponquogue Beach, Shinnecock Inlet

Hampton Bays is one of the liveliest of the summer communities of Long Island's east end. Just west of the Shinnecock Canal—the narrow channel separating the Montauk peninsula from the rest of Long Island—it is in a sense the gateway to the summer playgrounds of the south fork. This ride explores this popular vacation area and the ocean beaches to which it is connected.

The ride starts from the parking area at the side of the Shinnecock Canal. From here you can see the swift-flowing stream connecting Great Peconic Bay to the north with Shinnecock Bay to the south. The canal is about ¾ mile long and features tidal gates that control the flow of water and a lock providing boat passage. The lock is necessary because the bays can differ in elevation by as much as 4 feet. The canal was completed in 1892, more than fifty years after it was first suggested to the state legislature.

From the canal we head north on Newtown Road, passing under Route 27, then west through a lightly developed wooded stretch at Canoe Place and Squiretown. The name Canoe Place reflects the historic Indian use of the area as a canoe portage route between the bays. Squiretown was once a center for salt-hay harvesting on Great Peconic Bay, an activity that attracted farming families from miles around during the cutting season. The terrain is fairly hilly in here,

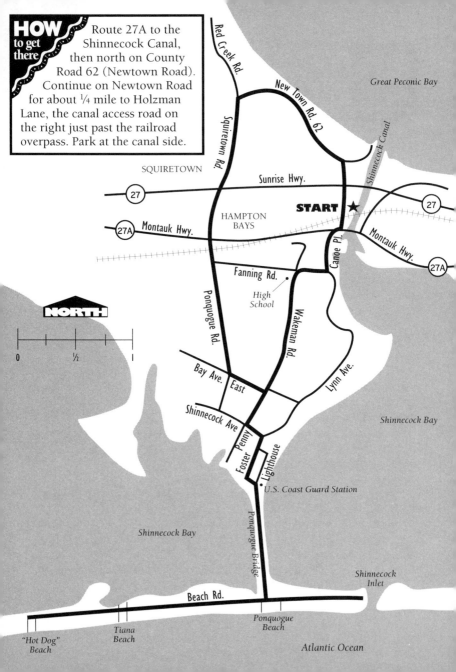

HOW to get there

Route 27A to the Shinnecock Canal, then north on County Road 62 (Newtown Road). Continue on Newtown Road for about ¼ mile to Holzman Lane, the canal access road on the right just past the railroad overpass. Park at the canal side.

Red Creek Rd.

New Town Rd. 62

Great Peconic Bay

Shinnecock Canal

Squiretown Rd.

SQUIRETOWN

Sunrise Hwy.

27

HAMPTON BAYS

START ★

27

27A Montauk Hwy.

Canoe Pl.

Montauk Hwy.

27A

Fanning Rd.

High School

Ponquogue Rd.

Wakeman Rd.

Lynn Ave.

NORTH

0   ½   1

Bay Ave.   East

Shinnecock Bay

Shinnecock Ave

Penny

Foster

Lighthouse

• U.S. Coast Guard Station

Shinnecock Bay

Ponquogue Bridge

Shinnecock Inlet

Beach Rd.

Ponquogue Beach

"Hot Dog" Beach

Tiana Beach

Atlantic Ocean

**DIREC-
TIONS
at a glance**

- From the canal road, proceed left on Gate Street one block to Newtown Road.
- Right on Newtown Road, passing under Route 27, then left at the T intersection for about 1¾ miles to its end at Red Creek–Squiretown Road.
- Left on Red Creek–Squiretown Road about 2¾ miles, past Routes 27, 27A, and the railroad tracks, onto Ponquogue Avenue to Bay Avenue East.
- Left on Bay Avenue East about ½ mile to Wakeman Road.
- Right on Wakeman Road to Shinnecock Avenue (at Penny Lane).
- Left on Shinnecock Avenue to Foster Avenue.
- Right on Foster Avenue about 1½ miles, over Ponquogue Bridge to Beach Road and Ponquogue Beach.
- Proceed east from Ponquogue Beach about 1 mile on Beach Road to Shinnecock Inlet.
- From Shinnecock Inlet return on Beach Road past Ponquogue Beach, continuing on about 1½ miles to Tiana Beach and another mile or so to "Hot Dog Beach."
- Return on Beach Road back to Ponquogue Beach, then back over the bridge to Foster Avenue, then back to Shinnecock Avenue.
- Left on Shinnecock Avenue to Wakeman Road.
- Right on Wakeman Road 1½ miles to Fanning Avenue, the third right past Hampton Bays High School.
- Right on Fanning to its end at Canoe Place Road–Lynn Avenue.
- Left on Canoe Place Road to Montauk Highway, Route 27A.
- Right on 27A to County Road 62 (Newtown Road).
- Left on Newtown Road under the railroad bridge to the canal access road and the ride starting point.

but there is little traffic, and the surroundings are attractive and quiet.

As we head south on Squiretown Road we enter Hampton Bays just south of Route 27. From here on, the atmosphere is one of a modern, busy, resort community. Most of the housing is devoted to that purpose and is in great demand, especially by singles' groups. In summer the place is crawling with sports cars, cyclists, and beach enthusiasts. South of Hampton Bays we proceed through the Ponquogue peninsula jutting into Shinnecock Bay, and then over Ponquogue Bridge to the ocean beach. The streets leading to the bridge and the bridge itself can be quite heavily trafficked in summer as the beach crowd comes and goes. The bridge is a two-lane structure with a pedestrian walk from which you get a good view of the bay stretching to the east and west.

At the end of the bridge at Beach Road, a road that runs the length of this section of the barrier beach from Shinnecock Inlet in the east to Moriches Inlet 15 miles to the west, we come to Ponquogue Beach, a broad stretch on the Atlantic offering swimming, rest rooms, and refreshments. If you are really hungry, however, wait until you get to Shinnecock Inlet, the next leg of the ride, where there are a couple of small, salty restaurants and marinas. Shinnecock Inlet itself is a fast-flowing run providing access to the Atlantic to the boaters on Shinnecock Bay. These small boats are usually present, fighting their way through the inlet if going against the flow or skimming in just barely under control if going with it. The inlet has existed only since 1938 when, during the great hurricane of that year, the ocean battered Long Island's south shore, cutting through the barrier beach at this point. There are usually a number of anglers on the rocks lining the inlet and a good crowd around the Coast Guard light.

We return from the inlet and head west past Ponquogue Beach to Tiana Beach and "Hot Dog Beach," a mile or so farther on. On summer weekends these places are jammed day and night, rain or shine, with hordes of partiers, mostly of college age. The music blasts from the local bars, and the convertible and dune-buggy traffic sometimes piles up and spills onto the sand shoulders of the road. It's a bit of southern California on Long Island and a great place for a beer.

From "Hot Dog Beach" and Tiana Beach we head back over the Ponquogue Bridge back through Ponquogue on Wakeman Road, a pleasant run through the communities traversed earlier. At the end of this leg we come to Canoe Place Road–Lynn Avenue, on which we return to Montauk Highway and the canal. This road is the main north-south artery in the area and should be cycled with care.

Southampton—North Sea

Number of miles:	24 (12 without the North Sea segment)
Approximate pedaling time:	4 hours (2 hours without the North Sea segment)
Terrain:	Flat in Southampton, hilly in North Sea segment
Surface:	Good; sandy in places
Traffic:	Heavy in village of Southampton, light to moderate elsewhere
Things to see:	St. Andrews Dune Church, Coopers Neck Beach, Shinnecock Inlet, Bullhead Bay, Settler's Monument, Southampton Village historic architecture

Southampton, with Southold on the north fork, is one of the oldest villages on Long Island. It dates from 1640 when a band of settlers, departing from Lynn, Massachusetts, arrived at North Sea on Great Peconic Bay. With great perseverance and some shrewd real estate dealings with the Shinnecock Indian tribe, they established a thriving community resting on strict Puritan principles of sobriety and dedication to work. They selected a beautiful place, including a beachfront on the Atlantic, fertile, flat woodlands, and access to the fish and shellfish of Shinnecock and Great Peconic bays.

The ride starts on Main Street and proceeds to the eastern parts of the village at Meeting House Lane and Old Town Road. Near the center of the village the houses are large, old, comfortable dwellings, wide-spaced and shaded with massive trees. As we approach the beach the style of architecture changes to sun-bleached cedar and white trim, but the quality of comfort remains. All along Gin Lane are large and attractive beachfront homes. These line the road along the

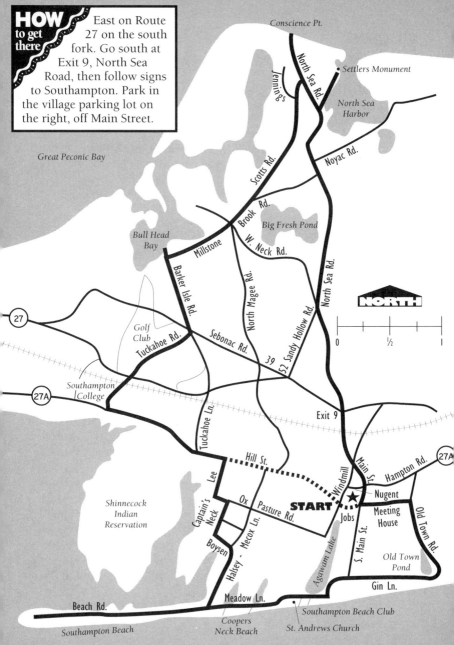

HOW to get there

East on Route 27 on the south fork. Go south at Exit 9, North Sea Road, then follow signs to Southampton. Park in the village parking lot on the right, off Main Street.

Conscience Pt.

Settlers Monument

North Sea Harbor

Jennings

North Sea Rd.

Noyac Rd.

Great Peconic Bay

Scotts Rd.

Brook Rd.

Big Fresh Pond

W. Neck Rd.

Millstone

Bull Head Bay

Barker Isle Rd.

North Magee Rd.

52 Sandy Hollow Rd.

North Sea Rd.

NORTH

0   ½   1

Golf Club

Tuckahoe Rd.

Sebonac Rd.

39

27

Southampton College

27A

Tuckahoe Ln.

Exit 9

Hill St.

Lee

Windmill

Main St.

Hampton Rd.

27A

Shinnecock Indian Reservation

Captain's Neck

Ox

Pasture Rd.

START

★

Nugent

Meeting House

Jobs

Boysen

Halsey - Mecox Ln.

Agawam Lake

S. Main St.

Old Town Rd.

Old Town Pond

Gin Ln.

Beach Rd.

Meadow Ln.

Coopers Neck Beach

St. Andrews Church

Southampton Beach Club

Southampton Beach

Atlantic Ocean

DIREC-TIONS at a glance

- From the village parking lot proceed right on Main Street to Meeting House Lane on the left, opposite Jobs Lane.
- Left on Meeting House Lane to Old Town Road.
- Right on Old Town Road to Gin Lane.
- Right on Gin Lane (Dune Road farther on) to Meadow Lane.
- Left on Meadow Lane onto Beach Road.
- Proceed on Beach Road and return for a 4-mile round-trip along Southampton Beach.
- Left on Halsey Neck Lane (first left) opposite beach parking lot, about ½ mile to Boysen Road.
- Left on Boysen Road to Captains Neck Lane.
- Right on Captains Neck Lane to Ox Pasture Road.
- Left on Ox Pasture Road to Lee Avenue.
- Right on Lee Avenue to Hill Street, Route 27A.
- Those wishing to return to Southampton, go right on Hill Street for about 1 mile to Jobs Lane, then on to Main Street. The full ride proceeds left on Hill Street about 1¼ miles to Tuckahoe Road (past Tuckahoe Lane) on the right.
- Right on Tuckahoe Road through Southampton College, over the railroad tracks and Route 27 (County Route 39) through the Shinnecock Hills Golf Club, to Sebonac Road–Barker Isle intersection.
- Proceed over Sebonac Road to Barker Isle Road, and continue on for about 1 mile to Bullhead Bay.
- Return from Bullhead Bay, then left onto Millstone Brook Road. Continue on Millstone Brook for about 1¼ miles, past the intersection with West Neck and North Magee roads, to Scotts Road, branching to the left from Millstone Brook.
- Continue on Scotts Road, bearing left at every intersection, to its end at North Sea Road.
- Left on North Sea Road to its end at Conscience Point Beach.
- Return on North Sea Road (Suffolk County Route 38) for about 1½ miles to Route 27. (About ½ mile past Scotts Road on the left is the Settlers Monument Path.)

- Continue on North Sea Road under the railroad tracks to the merge with Main Street. Continue on Main to the ride starting point in the village parking lot.

---

beach for most of the ride. At Agawam Lake we come to the Southampton Beach Club, a busy center of tennis and swimming, and just beyond it the St. Andrews Dune Church, built in the late 1800s, an interesting, heavy, dark-red building somewhat out of place here. Opposite it, Agawam Lake offers a tranquil water view that contrasts nicely with the oceanfront, being a calm, tree-lined, and generally green spot in this otherwise bright, sandy area.

About a mile along we get an opportunity to view and swim the Atlantic at Coopers Neck Beach. In addition to the breakers it offers a refreshment stand and rest rooms. Beyond Coopers Neck Beach is the beginning of a 2-mile-long run along Southampton Beach. The road ends at Shinnecock Inlet, with a great view of Shinnecock Bay to the north. All along this road are spectacular beach dwellings for which Southampton is known. From the beach road we head north through additional comfortable and pleasant streets, finally reaching Hill Street (Route 27A). We go west on Hill Street past the Shinnecock Indian reservation on the left, where cyclists are not welcome, to Tuckahoe Road. We proceed north on Tuckahoe through Southampton College, then over the railroad tracks to Route 27 (County Route 39). Next we proceed across this road with care (the two-way traffic is usually extremely heavy) and then through the Shinnecock Hills Golf Club, site of the 1995 PGA United States Open, to the beginning of a run through the hillier and more wooded sections of North Sea. At the end of Barker Isle Road is Bullhead Bay, an attractive sheltered inlet usually harboring a number of small boats, from which we proceed 2½ miles through hilly pleasant country. The road is lined with stands of oak covered in places with shrouds of catbrier. There are very few homes in the area so that it is one of those increasingly rare stretches where natural Long Island vegetation can be viewed quietly, close-up, and in some abundance.

At its end we come to North Sea Road, where we head north to Conscience Point. A road marker indicates the way to the landing site of the original Southampton settlers. A plaque on a large boulder at water's edge commemorates the event. At the end of North Sea Road is a beach at which swimming is allowed but at which no amenities are provided. The view, however, is striking looking out over Peconic Bay to Robins Island on the left and Little Hog Neck on the north fork directly opposite. We return to Southampton on North Sea Road, which is rather unspectacular and also has some traffic.

There are several interesting historical sites in the village that might be of interest after the ride. These include the Elias Pelletreau Silver Shop (c. 1750) on Main Street near Cameron Street; the Southampton Historical Museum at Main and Meeting House Lane; the Halsey House Museum (c. 1650) on South Main Street; and Hollyhocks (c. 1650) at Main and Foster streets.

Bridgehampton— Water Mill

Number of miles:	20 (12 miles for short ride through Bridgehampton)
Approximate pedaling time:	4 hours (short ride 2 hours)
Terrain:	Flat
Surface:	Good; sandy in places
Traffic:	Light
Things to see:	Berwind Memorial, Hedges Homestead, Water Mill Village Green, Old Water Mill Museum, Bridgehampton Historical Museum

Halfway between Southampton and Easthampton lies Bridgehampton, and a few miles west of it, the village of Water Mill. In the hierarchy of vacation spots on Long Island's south fork, Bridgehampton rates somewhere between those venerable communities and Westhampton and Hampton Bays. Bridgehampton differs from the others, however, in that it seems to have an identity independent of its summer-resort image. Just a short distance from the village center are open, rich farmlands that surround the community, stretching south to the ocean beaches and north to the center of the peninsula. While Bridgehampton has its share of expensive summer housing, a closer look finds it to be a prosperous farming area. This ride tours both the farms and the playgrounds and some of the interesting historical sites along the way.

The ride starts from the village center and proceeds south on Ocean Road to Sagaponack Road, past the Berwind Memorial, a windmill built around 1830 and moved several times before arriving at its present location. We head west on Sagaponack and once past the Bridgehampton Golf Club come to the beginning of farmland.

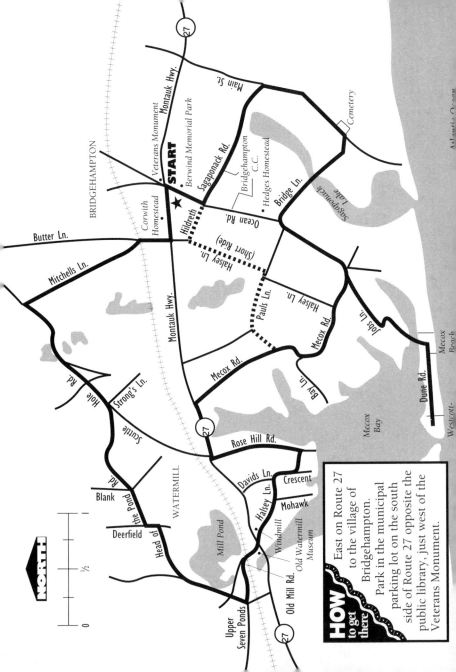

- Go right from the parking lot on Route 27 to Ocean Road at the Veterans Monument.
- Right on Ocean Road, past the Berwind Memorial Park, to Sagaponack Road on the left.
- Left on Sagaponack Road past the Bridgehampton Golf Club about 1½ miles to Main Street.
- Right at Main Street about 1 mile to Bridge Lane.
- Right on Bridge Lane, over Sagaponack Lake Bridge, to Ocean Road. Hedges Homestead is on the right.
- Left on Ocean Road about 1 mile to Mecox Road.
- Right on Mecox ¼ mile to Jobs Lane on the left.
- Left on Jobs Lane to its end at Mecox Beach, then right on Dune Road to Westcott-Cameron Beach, a distance of about 2 miles. Return on Dune Road and Jobs Lane to Mecox Road.
- Left on Mecox Road for about 2 miles (bearing right at Bay Lane ¼ mile along) to Route 27 (Montauk Highway). Those wishing to return to Bridgehampton can go right on Paul's Lane, the first right past Bay Lane, then right at the unmarked intersection to Halsey Lane on the left. Go left on Halsey Lane to Hildreth Lane, then right to Ocean Road, then left back to Montauk Highway (Route 27).
- Left on Route 27 about ½ mile to Rose Hill Road on the left.
- Left on Rose Hill Road about 1 mile to its end at Mecox Bay.
- From Mecox Bay go left on Halsey Lane for about 1 mile to Route 27 at the windmill.
- Jog left on Route 27 to Old Mill Road on the right.
- Right on Old Mill Road, with the Old Water Mill Museum on the left, over the railroad tracks to Upper Seven Ponds Road.
- Left on Upper Seven Ponds Road to Head of Pond Road.
- Right on Head of Pond Road for about 3 miles (going left at Deerfield Lane) to the merge with Scuttlehole Road at Strongs Lane.
- Go left on Scuttlehole Road for about 1½ miles, past the ponds to Mitchells Lane.

- Right on Mitchells Lane about 1½ miles to the merge with Butter Lane at the railroad overpass, then continue right on Butter Lane under the overpass to Route 27.
- Left on Route 27, with the Bridgehampton Historical Museum on the left, about ½ mile to the ride starting point.

The farms have been altered at their edges somewhat by the building of year-round homes, which themselves appear quite substantial. This pattern of farms and new homes exists throughout the area south of the village.

After crossing over Sagaponack Lake, a beautiful, narrow sheet of calm water, we turn south at Ocean Road. On the right at the Bridge Lane-Ocean Road intersection is the Hedges Homestead, built in the mid-1700s. At Mecox Road we follow the signs to the town beaches. Heading out on Jobs Lane we see the first of the modern beach-home architecture common in the wealthier sections of the south fork. In contrast to the older-style homes of dark cedar bordered with white trim, these are stark and gaunt, in pale shades of gray with flashes of glass and plastic. They are located in unprotected open sand stretches and knolls, appearing somewhat forlorn in their sleek efficiency.

At the end of Jobs Lane we come to Mecox Beach on the open Atlantic. Just over the high dunes can be seen the crashing breakers of the ocean, white froth on pale green water—a great sight. A mile or so farther along on Dune Road is Westcott-Cameron Beach, another opening to the Atlantic. The ride out and back to Westcott provides an excellent view of more beach homes and Mecox Bay and Water Mill to the north. Refreshments and rest rooms are available at the pavilion on the dunes.

From the beaches we head north on Mecox Road through 2 miles or so of tranquil farms and homes, at the end of which is Montauk Highway (Route 27). The next half mile requires riding on the shoulder of this heavily trafficked road, but at Rose Hill Road we enter peaceful farm country once again at Water Mill. At the end of Rose Hill Road is an opening to Mecox Bay, providing an excellent view of that body, and in the distance the beach dunes we previously cycled past. At the end of Halsey Lane we come again to Montauk Highway at the Water Mill village green, with its windmill landmark built around 1800.

The shops along Montauk Highway have been remodeled in the manner of a colonial village and are quite attractive. We proceed over Montauk Highway onto Upper Seven Ponds Road to the Old Water Mill Museum. This mill was built in 1644 and has been restored so that it can once again grind the corn and grains grown in the area. Power is supplied as it always has been, by the quiet flow from Mill Pond just north of the museum. Demonstrations of grinding are given every day. In addition there are displays of tools and instruments used by the early settlers and colonists.

The remainder of the ride goes through 5 miles of productive farmland, a great deal of it grass sod that will end up on the lawns of Nassau County. As we return to the center of the village and the ride starting point we pass on the left the Bridgehampton Historical Museum, housed in the August Corwith Homestead, built around 1770.

Sag Harbor—North Haven

Number of miles:	13
Approximate pedaling time:	2 hours
Terrain:	Hilly
Surface:	Generally good; rough in some places
Traffic:	Heavy in village
Things to see:	Shelter Island Ferry landing, Foster Memorial Beach, Sag Harbor Whaling Museum, Whalers Church

Sag Harbor was Long Island's center of whaling for half a century during the early and mid-1800s. After a crude start on the beaches of Southampton and Easthampton, where whales often beached and were thus easily taken, residents of Long Island's eastern end went to sea from Sag Harbor and joined the great American whaling fleet. With Nantucket, New Bedford, and New London, Sag Harbor prospered from the lucrative whale hunts. It is estimated that as many as sixty whaling vessels were based in Sag Harbor in 1847, at the zenith of the town's whaling activity. With the coming of petroleum-based oil, however, the demand for whale oil gradually dwindled, as did the fortunes of Sag Harbor. The last whaling ship left port in 1874.

This heritage is both tangible and visible in the setting, architecture, and nautical atmosphere of the village. Overlying it all is the ambience of a summer recreation center—much like its counterpart villages on the south shore and the eastern end of the north fork. Sag Harbor offers, in addition to its exceptionally scenic location, a variety of restaurants, bookstores, antique shops, and other attractions that make it a perfect place to end a day's riding.

The ride starts on Main Street and proceeds north from the village. At the base of Main Street we cross the bridge to North Haven

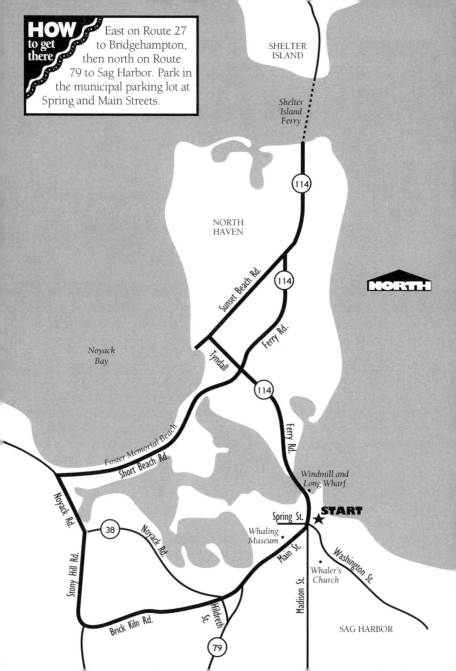

HOW to get there

East on Route 27 to Bridgehampton, then north on Route 79 to Sag Harbor. Park in the municipal parking lot at Spring and Main Streets.

SHELTER ISLAND

Shelter Island Ferry

114

NORTH HAVEN

Sunset Beach Rd.

114

Ferry Rd.

NORTH

Noyack Bay

Tyndall

114

Foster Memorial Beach

Short Beach Rd.

Ferry Rd.

Windmill and Long Wharf

Spring St. ★ **START**

Noyack Rd.

38

Noyack Rd.

Stony Hill Rd.

Whaling Museum

Main St.

Washington St.

Whaler's Church

Madison St.

Brick Kiln Rd.

Hildreth St.

79

SAG HARBOR

DIREC-TIONS at a glance

- From the parking lot at Spring and Main Streets, go left on Main to Long Wharf and the Windmill.
- Proceed right onto Route 114 (Ferry Road) over the bridge to North Haven on the designated sideway shoulder. Continue on Ferry Road for about 3 miles to its end at the Shelter

Island ferry landing. Those wishing to ride on Shelter Island can use the Shelter Island directions. (Ride 26)

- Return on Route 114 about 1¼ miles to the Sunset Beach Road turnoff to the right at the "114 South" sign.
- Continue on Sunset Beach Road for about 1 mile to its end at Noyack Bay.
- Return on Sunset Beach Road one block to Tyndall Road on the right.
- Right on Tyndall Road to Short Beach Road, to the right at the Route 114 intersection.
- Right at Short Beach Road for about 2 miles along Noyack Bay, past Foster Memorial Beach, to the end of the road at the Noyack Road (Route 38) intersection.
- Left on Noyack Road, continuing onto Stony Hill Road for about 1¾ miles to Brick Kiln Road.
- Left on Brick Kiln Road, past Hildreth Street, to Main Street at Mashashimuet Park.
- Left on Main Street for about 1 mile to the ride starting point.

---

and view along the way Gardiners Bay to the east and Sag Harbor Cove to the west. It was these sheltered bodies of water that provided safe harbor for the whalers, who were away for long periods of time—often for three years or more.

The ride traverses North Haven on the designated sideway shoulder along Ferry Road for a distance of about 3 miles through a pleasant area of established and well-tended homes. At the end of Ferry Road can be seen the Shelter Island ferries, small, open-ended boats that constantly ply the narrow crossing. (The ferry landing on Shelter Island is a terminal point for the Shelter Island bike ride.)

We return from the ferry landing along Ferry Road for a short distance to Sunset Beach Road, which runs for about a mile to Noyack Bay. This is an exceptionally pleasant leg, passing through a quiet, tree-lined area and ending at a small, pebbly beach providing a terrific view of the bay.

The next leg of the ride, on Short Beach Road, follows the bay shoreline along Foster Memorial Beach, an easy 2-mile run that offers an excellent view of the bay and an opportunity for swimming. At the end of Short Beach Road on the left is a historical marker describing a Revolutionary War skirmish that occurred at the site.

The ride turns south on Noyack Road at this point and begins the return to the village. The riding is more difficult from here on because of the more challenging terrain. Noyack Road itself has narrow shoulders and presents a fairly steep hill climb. Some auto traffic can be expected as well. At Brick Kiln Road, however, where the ride turns left, a long downhill run begins that takes us back into the village center. Along Brick Kiln Road are large modern houses that contrast sharply with the historic architecture of the village. The ride turns left on Main Street at Masashimuet Park, with its striking Veterans' Monument, for a 1-mile run to the starting point.

The Sag Harbor village center is a National Historic District and boasts dozens of architectural gems, some of which date from colonial times. A guide to the village that details twenty-five distinctive structures can be obtained from the Chamber of Commerce office in the windmill at the foot of Main Street. Of special interest are the Sag Harbor Whaling Museum (c. 1850), a Greek Revival structure at Main and Garden streets, known for its collection of whaling artifacts and nautical histories; and the Whaler's Church (c. 1840), an outstanding example in wood of Egyptian Revival architecture.

East Hampton—
Amagansett

Number of miles:	17 (29 with Springs-Fireplace Loop)
Approximate pedaling time:	3 hours (7 with Springs-Fireplace Loop)
Terrain:	Flat in East Hampton–Amagansett, some hills in Springs–Fireplace Loop
Surface:	Good; sandy in places
Traffic:	Heavy on Main Street, East Hampton, light elsewhere
Things to see:	East Hampton Town Marine Museum, Beach Hampton, Gerard Drive peninsula on Gardiners Bay

The village of East Hampton is the easternmost of the Hampton communities of the south fork. It is an old and extremely attractive place rich in historical sights, enhanced with a location on the open Atlantic. In addition to the beachfront, the community contains a number of attractive ponds and lakes and is surrounded in part by pleasant expanses of farms. To the north is a hillier area, mostly tree-covered, with here and there a small farm, that runs to Gardiners Bay, along which are numerous ragged and irregular small inlets and harbors.

The ride consists of two segments: the basic ride, running through East Hampton, Amagansett, and the Atlantic beaches, and a northern loop running to Gardiners Bay through the communities of Springs and Fireplace. The northern loop more than doubles the length of the ride and goes through a moderately hilly area, but for those up to it, it makes an excellent whole-day bicycling outing.

The ride begins from the eastern end of East Hampton Village and proceeds south toward the beach on Egypt Lane. Along this road are

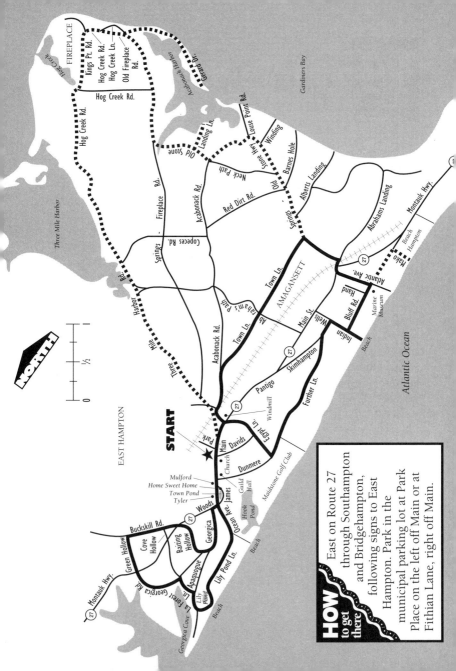

NORTH

THREE MILE HARBOR

HOG CREEK

FIREPLACE

Kings Pt. Rd.
Hog Creek Rd.
Hog Creek Ln.
Old Fireplace Rd.

Hog Creek Rd.

Hog Creek Rd.

Gerard Dr.

Acabonack Harbor

Gardiners Bay

Louse Point Rd.

Landing Ln.

Old Stone Hwy.

Winding

Barnes Hole

Neck Path

Red Dirt Rd.

Fireplace Rd.

Acabonack Rd.

Springs - Fireplace Rd.

Copeces Rd.

Springs

Harbor Rd.

Three Mile Harbor Rd.

Acabonack Rd.

Town Ln.

Alberts Landing

Springs

Abrahams Landing

Montauk Hwy.

Beach Hampton

27

Mako

Atlantic Ave.

AMAGANSETT

Abraham's Path

Hand

Bluff Rd.

Marine Museum

Indian

Beach

Main St.

Wells

Skimhampton

27

Pantigo

Further Ln.

Windmill

Egypt Ln.

27

Town Ln.

EAST HAMPTON

START

Main

Davids

Church

Dunmere

Mulford
Home Sweet Home
Town Pond
Tyler

Woods

Ocean Ave. James

Guild Hall

Hook Pond

Maidstone Golf Club

Atlantic Ocean

Beach

Buckskill Rd.

27

Green Hollow

Cove Hollow

Baiting Hollow

Georgica

Apaquogue

Lily Pond Ln.

La Forest Georgica Rd.

Lily Pond Ln.

Beach

Georgica Cove

Montauk Hwy.

27

HOW to get there

East on Route 27 through Southampton and Bridgehampton, following signs to East Hampton. Park in the municipal parking lot at Park Place on the left off Main or at Fithian Lane, right off Main.

0   ½   1 Mile

- Go east from the parking lot on Main Street toward the windmill to Egypt Lane on the right.
- Right on Egypt Lane about 1 mile to its end, at the Maidstone Golf Club, then left at Dunmere onto Further Lane.
- Proceed on Further Lane for about 2¼ miles, past the merge with Skimhampton Road to Indian Wells Highway.
- Right on Indian Wells to its end at Indian Wells Beach.
- From the beach go right on Bluff Road past the East Hampton Town Marine Museum, about ¾ mile, to Atlantic Avenue. (Beach Hampton, about a mile east of here, can be entered at Mako Road.)
- Left on Old Atlantic Avenue about ¾ mile to Montauk Highway (Route 27).
- Right on Montauk Highway for one block, bearing left over the railroad tracks to Old Stone Highway on the left.
- Left on Old Stone Highway about ¾ mile to Town Lane on the left.
- Left on Town Lane for about 2¼ miles to Acabonack Road. (The Springs-Fireplace Loop starts here; see directions following those for the basic ride.)
- Left on Acabonack Road for about 1 mile; then bear left under the railroad overpass to Pantigo Road. (The Springs-Fireplace Loop rejoins the basic ride here.)
- Right on Pantigo Road (Main Street) past the ride starting point about 1¼ miles through the village of East Hampton to Ocean Avenue, across the intersection at which Route 27 turns right.
- Continue on Ocean Avenue for about ¾ mile to Lily Pond Lane on the right.
- Right on Lily Pond Lane for about 1½ miles to Apaquogue Road.
- Right on Apaquogue Road to La Forest Lane on the left.
- Left on La Forest to its end at Georgica Road.
- Left on Georgica Road past Georgica Cove about ¾ mile to Montauk Highway (Route 27), going right at the fork.
- Proceed over Route 27, jogging left onto Green Hollow Road, then continue on for ½ mile to Buckskill Road.

- Right on Buckskill Road for about ¾ mile over Route 27, to its end at Baiting Hollow Road.
- Right on Baiting Hollow Road for ½ mile to Georgica Road.
- Left on Georgica Road about ¾ mile to Woods Lane, Route 27.
- Right on Woods Lane, following Route 27 west through the village to the ride starting point on Main Street.

Springs-Fireplace Loop:

- From Old Stone Highway at Town Lane, proceed right on Springs–Old Stone Highway Road.
- Continue on Springs–Old Stone Highway for 2½ miles to Neck Path.
- Right at Neck Path, continuing on Old Stone Highway past Acabonack Road, for about 1 mile to Springs-Fireplace Road.
- Right on Springs–Fireplace Road about 1¾ miles to Gerard Drive on the right.
- Right on Gerard Drive for about a 3-mile round-trip on Gerard Peninsula, enclosing Acabonack Harbor.
- Go right from Gerard Drive on Old Fireplace Road to Hog Creek Lane.
- Left on Hog Creek Lane about ½ mile to Kings Point Road.
- Left on Kings Point Road about ¾ mile to Hog Creek Road.
- Right on Hog Creek Road, which becomes Three Mile Harbor Road, for about 5¼ miles to the merge with North Main Street in East Hampton village.
- Continue on North Main Street, under the railroad overpass to Pantigo Road. Follow the basic ride from here.

typical summer homes for which East Hampton is famous—luxurious mansions of weathered cedar on large manicured lawns shaded by tall graceful trees. At the end of Egypt Lane is the Maidstone Club, dating from the late 1800s, with its open vistas of clipped fairways. We proceed east from here along Further Lane for about 2 miles, through an area of farms and pleasant homes to Indian Wells Road, where we turn south to the beach. The ocean air is exhilarating and the surf enticing on hot days. For contrast, try to imagine earlier times when East Hampton colonists worked the dunes searching for beached whales. When found, such whales were cut and dried right on the beach, a profitable and common occurrence then.

We return from the beach on Indian Wells Road and continue east on Bluff Road. From here we get a panoramic view of the grass-covered dunes and several small homes standing forlornly on them. Opposite Hand Lane, on the right, is the East Hampton Town Marine Museum, featuring displays of south fork fishing processes and whaling history. We turn north at Atlantic Avenue, but it might be of interest to observe the community of Beach Hampton about a mile or so farther east on the beach, to see the results of modern beachfront development. The expensive and ultramodern beach homes are jammed so closely together that a claustrophobic quality is created that completely destroys the open beach atmosphere that most people come here for. It is a congested suburban cluster at the ocean's edge, startlingly different from the older East Hampton.

We proceed north on Atlantic Avenue to Main Street, Amagansett, then right over the railroad tracks, entering farm country at Old Stone Highway. Here and along Town Lane back to East Hampton we are in the agricultural working land of the area. While there are some summer residences, most of the land is devoted to farming or is undeveloped. We turn south from Town Lane on Old Acabonack Road, proceed through a neighborhood of small homes and commercial establishments, and arrive back on Pantigo Lane–Main Street in East Hampton.

East Hampton dates from 1648 when the first English settlers arrived from Massachusetts. After purchasing the land from the Montauk Indians, at a bargain price in clothing and tools (valued at the time at about thirty pounds, the annual pay of a schoolmaster), they formed a close-knit, industrious Puritan community. They thrived on farming and fishing but remained secluded and distant until the charms of the village were noticed by those wealthy individuals of the mid-1800s who had the wherewithal to travel this far to escape the heat and dust of New York City in summer. The village be-

came a center for wealthy summer vacationists and remained an exclusive and remote compound until the railroad and improved road system reached it at the turn of the century. Even then it remained a place for more well-to-do vacationers. The village still displays an air of substance with its broad and opulent main streets with large homes, expensive shops, and tanned, well-dressed pedestrians.

Along Main Street are several well-preserved historical structures and homes. At the east end is the Old Hook mill, built in 1806. Farther west in the village center along Main Street is the Presbyterian Church, on the left just past Davids Lane, built in 1860. At Dunmere Lane is Guild Hall on the left and Clinton Academy on the right. Guild Hall houses an extensive collection of paintings by artists who at one time lived in East Hampton; Clinton Academy, a restored eighteenth-century school building, displays historical items from East Hampton and its surrounding communities. Farther on, on James Lane on the left, is the Mulford House and the Home Sweet Home Museum. Both these buildings date from the seventeenth century, the latter commemorating the composer John Howard Payne. We continue on past Town Pond where at 217 Main Street can be seen the residence used by President John Tyler during a visit to Long Island in 1845.

We continue west and away from the village center and proceed on Ocean Avenue, Lily Pond Road, and Georgica Avenue through an area of extremely large and fashionable homes. The neighborhood changes abruptly at Montauk Highway where we begin a short leg along Green Hollow and Buckskill roads, through a rural working area. We reenter the village on Woods Lane, where some traffic can be expected, and proceed back on Main Street to the ride starting point.

The northern loop through the communities of Springs and Fireplace provides a pleasant ramble through a very lightly developed area to the north shore of the peninsula on Gardiners Bay. The loop starts at Old Stone Highway and Town Lane and proceeds north on Old Stone Highway. The road is lined with densely treed sections alternating with small homesites. On Gerard Drive we run to the end of a narrow peninsula that encloses Acabonack Harbor. Out in

Gardiners Bay is Gardiners Island, visible to the northeast. The island was purchased from the Montauk Indians by Lyon Gardiner in 1639, becoming the first English settlement in what is now New York State. We proceed from here through Fireplace and then south past Three Mile Harbor. The ride from Three Mile Harbor south to East Hampton runs through a nondescript mix of light woods, small homes, and commercial establishments, with increasing traffic as you approach the village. We rejoin the basic ride route at Pantigo Road and North Main Street.

Montauk

Number of miles:	17 (25 with Hither Hills State Park Loop)
Approximate pedaling time:	4 hours (6 hours with Hither Hills Loop)
Terrain:	Moderately hilly
Surface:	Good; sandy in places
Traffic:	Heavy in Montauk, moderate elsewhere
Things to see:	Montauk Point Lighthouse, Oyster Pond Overlook, Star Island, Hither Hills State Park

Montauk is the easternmost extremity of the south fork, reaching 120 miles into the Atlantic from New York City. It is a narrow peninsula, hilly in places, with a constant sea breeze and clear, clean air. The Atlantic beats along its beaches on its southern edge, and Block Island Sound intrudes in several bays and inlets along its north shore. Its developed areas include Montauk Beach near Hither Hills State Park at the western end and Montauk village and Ditch Plains near its center. The eastern end, unpopulated, is devoted to state and county park use, a small Air Force radar station, and, at the very tip of the peninsula, the famous Montauk Point lighthouse station.

We proceed east from the village center on Montauk Point State Parkway (Route 27) toward Montauk Point. This road can have appreciable traffic, but the shoulder is wide and smooth and the hills long and gentle. Once past the populated sections of Ditch Plains and Lake Montauk, we come to the open country that once served as a grazing area for great herds of cattle. Every year they were brought in from western Long Island for fattening. The cattle were tended by in-

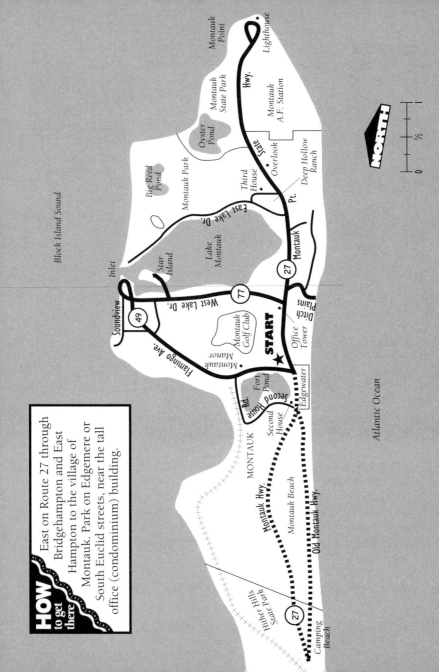

HOW to get there

East on Route 27 through Bridgehampton and East Hampton to the village of Montauk. Park on Edgemere or South Euclid streets, near the tall office (condominium) building.

NORTH

0   ½   1

Block Island Sound

Atlantic Ocean

Montauk Point

Lighthouse

Hwy.

Montauk State Park

Montauk A.F. Station

Oyster Pond

State

Overlook

Deep Hollow Ranch

Big Reed Pond

Montauk Park

Third House

Pt.

East Lake Dr.

Montauk

27

Lake Montauk

Star Island

Inlet

Soundview

49

West Lake Dr.

77

Flamingo Ave.

Montauk Golf Club

Montauk Manor

START

Office Tower

Ditch Plains

Edgewater

Fort Pond

Second House Rd.

Second House

MONTAUK

Montauk Hwy.

Montauk Beach

Old Montauk Hwy.

27

Hither Hills State Park

Camping Beach

- From Edgemere and South Euclid streets, proceed left to Montauk Point State Parkway (Route 27), then left again for about 5½ miles past Third House and the overlook to Montauk Point and the lighthouse.
- Return on Route 27 about 4½ miles to Ditch Plains Road on the left.
- Left on Ditch Plains Road for about ½ mile to the beach and back.
- Go left on Route 27 ¼ mile to West Lake Drive (Route 77) on the right.
- Right on West Lake Drive about 1¾ miles to Star Island turnoff.
- Right onto Star Island and return.
- Continue north on West Lake Drive to the Lake Montauk inlet parking area.
- From the inlet proceed south on Route 49 (Flamingo Avenue) 3½ miles, past Montauk Manor, onto Edgemere Road. Continue to the ride starting point at South Euclid Street.

Hither Hills State Park Loop:

- Proceed west from the ride starting point about ½ mile on Route 27 (Montauk Highway) to the Old Montauk Highway turnoff on the left, just past Second House Museum.
- Continue on Old Montauk Highway for about 3½ miles to Hither Hills State Park camping and swimming beach.
- Return on Old Montauk Highway or on Route 27 (Montauk Highway).

dividuals, appointed by the company that owned the land, who lived in the only three houses on the peninsula. Third House, the most easterly of the three, on the left just past East Lake Drive and Deep Hollow Ranch, was built in 1806, replacing a structure built in 1749. In 1898 Third House and the surrounding fields were used as a quarantine area for Theodore Roosevelt and 30,000 other U.S. Army troops just returned from the Spanish-American War.

About a mile along on the right is an overlook from which you get a good view of the hills of the point, Oyster Pond across the way, and Block Island Sound with Rhode Island in the distance. At the end of Route 27 is Montauk Point State Park and the lighthouse. The lighthouse stands 100 feet tall on a cliff on Turtle Cove, putting the light 170 feet above sea level. There are, of course, excellent views of the turbulent race where the waters of the Atlantic and Block Island Sound meet east of the point. The lighthouse, built in 1795, was originally placed about 300 feet from the cliff edge. Since that time the ocean has eaten away at the point to the extent that it is almost lapping at the foundations of the light. In time, no doubt, the light will have to be moved inland.

We return to Montauk with a short diversion to the beach at Ditch Plains, a small community of beach homes, and then proceed north on West Lake Drive. About 2 miles along on the right is the Star Island turnoff, from which you get a good view of Lake Montauk and its inlet on Block Island Sound. We continue north to the inlet itself where we find the major activity of Montauk: the fishers, commercial and recreational, who can be seen going through the inlet in a continuous parade of boats of all kinds. The neighborhood abounds in restaurants, fish dealers, marinas, and boatyards. There is no more briny place in all Long Island.

Proceeding south from the inlet, about halfway along on Flamingo Road we pass the eastern terminus of the Long Island Railroad. On the left at the top of a hill is Montauk Manor, which, with the tall office tower (now a residential condominium complex) in the center of the village, is the remains of an ill-fated attempt to develop Montauk as the "Miami of the north" in the 1920s. Swimming beaches are located near the village center on South Edgewater Avenue, running for several blocks on the Atlantic.

We proceed west from the village center on Route 27 for a loop through Hither Hills State Park. We pass Second House Museum, built in 1746, on the right at Second House Road, and we turn left just past this onto Old Montauk Highway. This is a curving, undulating, bumpy road that provides an excellent view of the ocean and the many attractive vacation homes built along its edge in the community of Montauk Beach. At its end is the picnic, swimming, and camping area of the park. Hither Hills consists of 1,755 acres, most of it in the woodlands to the north. You can cycle through these beautiful stretches of oak by returning to Montauk on Route 27.

Shelter Island

Number of miles:	Basic ride—18; southern loop—5; western loop—7; total—30
Approximate pedaling time:	Basic ride—4 hours; southern loop—1 hour; western loop—2 hours; total—7 hours
Terrain:	Hilly in northern sections, flat elsewhere
Surface:	Good; some sections rough-surfaced and sandy
Traffic:	Moderate on Route 114, light elsewhere
Things to see:	Shelter Island Ferry, Ram Island Drive, osprey nests, Sylvester Manor Windmill, Crescent Beach

Shelter Island is a 4-by-6-mile, randomly shaped plug located between Long Island's north and south forks, almost connecting the two. It faces Peconic Bay to the west and Gardiners Bay to the east, with narrow channels separating it from Greenport on the north and North Haven on the south. It is generally hilly but contains beautiful wooded areas, usually associated with the north shore of Long Island, and miles of beaches and superb water views. Except for the main north-south road, Route 114, it has little traffic, and there are no sections of the island that would be considered heavily developed. It is, in fact, a very quiet and conservative community. The population of about 1,700 people increases in the summer, but not excessively, and it contains few amusements beyond the extremely attractive scenery of water, woods, and homes. Even its history is somewhat subdued compared to the rich variety of neighboring Southold and the Hamptons. Not much remains of its colonial past in the way of structures and historical items, perhaps

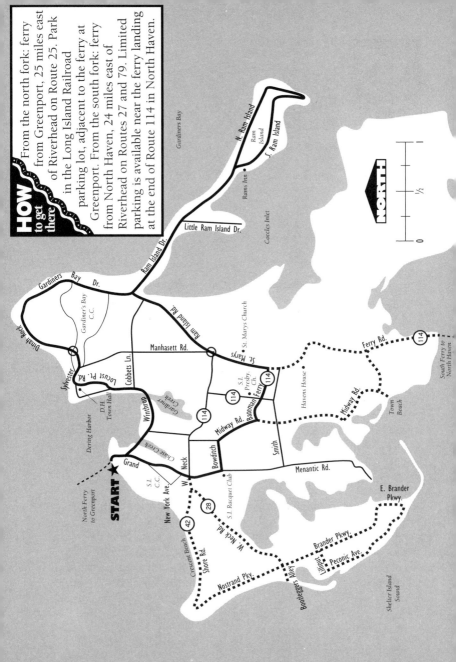

HOW to get there

From the north fork: ferry from Greenport, 25 miles east of Riverhead on Route 25. Park in the Long Island Railroad parking lot, adjacent to the ferry at Greenport. From the south fork: ferry from North Haven, 24 miles east of Riverhead on Routes 27 and 79. Limited parking is available near the ferry landing at the end of Route 114 in North Haven.

NORTH

0   ½   1

Gardiners Bay

W. Ram Island
Ram Island
S. Ram Island

Rams Inn

Coecles Inlet

Little Ram Island Dr.

Ram Island Dr.

Gardiners Bay Dr.

Gardiner's Bay C.C.

Dinah Rock

Sylvester

St. Marys Church

Manhasset Rd.

Ram Island Rd.

Locust Pt. Rd.

Cobbets Ln.

St. Marys

114

Ferry Rd.

114

South Ferry to North Haven

Havens House

S.I. Presby. Ch.

114

Bateman

Midway Rd.

Town Beach

Gardiner Creek

D.H. Town Hall

Winthrop

114

Midway Rd.

Ferry

Dering Harbor

Chase Creek

Neck

Bowditch

Smith

Menantic Rd.

Grand

★ START

S.I. C.C.

W. Neck Ave.

New York Ave.

E. Brander Pkwy.

North Ferry to Greenport

28

S.I. Racquet Club

42

W. Neck Rd.

Brander Pkwy.

Crescent Beach

Shore Rd.

Nostrand Pkwy.

Bootleggers Alley

Lilliput

Peconic Ave.

Shelter Island Sound

- From the ferry landing at Summerfield Road, follow Route 114 South on Grand and Chase avenues over Chase Creek to Winthrop Road on
the left.
- Continue on Winthrop Road, with Dering Harbor
on the left, over Gardiner Creek to the village of
Dering Harbor, just past Cobbetts Lane.
- Go right onto Locust Point Road, and continue on for about ½ mile
to Sylvester Road, just past the Dering Harbor Town Hall.
- Right on Sylvester Road for several hundred yards, then right again
at the road entrance to the Gardiners Bay Country Club on the left.
- Left through the club on Dinah Rock Road to the traffic circle, then
left, continuing on Dinah Rock Road.
- Continue on Dinah Rock Road for about 2 miles to Ram Island
Drive (Dinah Rock becomes Gardiners Bay Drive about a quarter of
the way along).
- Proceed out to Ram Island and return on Ram Island, North Ram
Island, and South Ram Island drives, about 6 miles round-trip.
- From Ram Island, turn left at Gardiners Bay Drive, continuing on
Ram Island Road for about 1¼ miles to the traffic circle.
- Left at the circle onto St. Mary's Road, then on for about ½ mile to
Ferry Road, Route 114.
- Right on 114 past the Shelter Island Presbyterian Church, then
straight ahead halfway around the circle onto Bateman Road.
- Continue on Bateman to Midway Road.
- Right on Midway about ½ mile to Bowditch Road on the left.
- Left on Bowditch to its end at Menantic Road at the Shelter Island
Racquet Club.
- Right on Menantic over West Neck Road (Route 28), onto New
York Avenue, with the Shelter Island Country Club on the left.
- Continue for about ½ mile on New York Avenue past Tower Hill
Road to Grand Avenue.
- Bear right on Grand Avenue and continue for ½ mile to
Summerfield Road and the ride starting point at the North Ferry.

Western Loop:

- From the Menantic-West Neck Road (Route 28) intersection, proceed west on West Neck onto Shore Road (Route 42), then on for 1¼ miles to its end at Nostrand Parkway. Crescent Beach is on the right.
- Follow Nostrand Parkway (Brander Parkway farther on) for 1½ miles to Lilliput Lane on the right.
- Right on Lilliput Lane to its end at Peconic Avenue.
- Left on Peconic Avenue for about 1 mile to North Brander Parkway.
- Left on North Brander, continuing onto Brander Parkway.
- Continue on Brander Parkway for about 1 mile to West Neck Road on the right, opposite Bootleggers Alley.
- Right on West Neck Road to its end at Shore Road.
- Right on Shore Road ¼ mile, connecting with the basic ride at Menantic Road.

Southern Loop:

- From St. Mary's Road, continue south on Ferry Road (Route 114), for about 2 miles to its end at the south ferry landing, passing Havens House on the right.
- Return on Ferry Road for about 1 mile to Midway Road on the left.
- Left on Midway for about 2 miles, connecting with the basic ride at Bateman Road.

---

because the island has always been sparsely populated. For the cyclist, however, it is a perfect place for a day's outing, especially when the pleasant ferry rides are added to the experience.

The ride consists of three parts: the basic ride covering the north central part of the island; a loop through the western parts; and a loop through the southern parts. The basic ride assumes the rider has come from Greenport; those coming from the south—from North Haven and Sag Harbor—can pick up the ride route through the southern loop.

After leaving the ferry from Greenport we proceed into Shelter Island Heights and immediately come to the hills that are found in the northern part of the island. This area is a melange of new and old homes, some dating from Victorian times, as evidenced by the ginger-bread facades and busy architecture of the older homes along Grand Avenue. We proceed through this area, probably the busiest on the is-land, and arrive at Chase Creek. Here we get the first of the several excellent views of the intricate harbors and inlets that exist on all sides of the island. To the north is Dering Harbor, with the Shelter Island Yacht Club on the left. Behind is Chase Creek, a typically quiet and serene backwater. Farther on we cross Gardiner Creek, with much the same view, and arrive at the village of Dering Harbor.

Dering Harbor is a community of expensive, well-tended homes shaded by massive trees, with terrific views of Dering Harbor, Shelter Island Sound, and Greenport. We pass through this attractive area and come to a more modern community at Dinah Rock Road, after traversing Gardiners Bay Country Club with its clipped fairways and greens. The homes along Dinah Rock are spaced wider apart and are lower and more rambling than those seen previously, but they remain quite attractive and maintain the water view. Many of the crossroads go to the water's edge, from which a broader view can be obtained.

At Ram Island Drive we come to a narrow 3-mile-long peninsula jutting into Gardiners Bay, encircling Coecles Harbor. Along this stretch we see in microcosm all the attributes of Shelter Island: treed and hilly terrain, pebbly, wind-blown beaches, and attractive homes. At the intersection of North and South Ram Island drives is the Rams Inn, an old, well-known lodging place. You will note on the stretches along the beaches the large stick-and-twig nests located on platforms on sawed-off utility poles. These are used by ospreys, beautiful birds reaching up to 3 feet in wingspan, that were once abundant here and in similar places on Long Island. Sometime in the past, however, they began to decrease in number, reportedly because of the effects of chemical pollutants in their food supply. However, the latest Audubon Society bird counts indicate that more of them are surviv-ing, lending hope that they will again populate the area to the extent they once did.

From Ram Island Drive we head inland on hilly terrain to the cen-ter of the island. On Manwaring Road, just west of Ram Island Road, is the Sylvester Manor Windmill, built around 1800. Just south is St.

Mary's Episcopal Church on the left. We turn west on Ferry Road and proceed to the center of the original Shelter Island settlement.

The first settlers arrived in 1652. By 1674, after a complicated series of sales, ownership of the island rested entirely with one Nathaniel Sylvester. The island was then subdivided several times, so that by 1730 ownership was spread among its twenty male inhabitants. It changed very slowly in the next two centuries, its population not exceeding 1,000 until the early 1920s. The site of the original settlement now contains a Presbyterian Church, founded in 1742, with the present building surrounded by cemeteries containing the graves of the early residents. From the village center we head west to Midway Road and then north on Menantic Road, back to Shelter Island Heights and the road back to the ferry.

The western loop begins where Menantic Road meets West Neck Road. We proceed west on Shore Road past Crescent Beach, a public swimming area with a beautiful water view, and proceed onto Nostrand Parkway. Along this leg and south on Peconic Avenue are some of the most attractive houses on Shelter Island. Some are new and of quite interesting design; others are large, comfortable, old weather-beaten structures. All command a striking view of Shelter Island Sound and, in the distance, Great Hog Neck. The way back goes past West Neck Bay, with more of the same comfortable and quiet scenery.

The southern loop starts from Ferry Road at the intersection with St. Mary's Road. We proceed south on Route 114 through an area of heavy woods and in some spots some commercial buildings and stores. About a mile along we come to Havens House, the former residence of the Havens family. It was built in the mid-1700s and is now maintained by the Shelter Island Historical Society. Continuing down Ferry Road we come to its end at the landing of the North Haven ferry. As in most other places on the island, the view of the racing water, passing boats, and shoreline homes is stunning. We proceed north on Midway Road from Ferry Road, passing the Shelter Island Town Beach, looking out over Shelter Island Sound, and farther on pass Menantic Creek on the left. The southern loop meets the basic ride at Bowditch Road.

Block Island

Number of miles:	Basic ride—9; north to Sachem Pond and return—8; total—17
Approximate pedaling time:	Basic ride—2 hours with stops; to Sachem Pond—1 hour; total—3 hours
Terrain:	Hilly on west and south sides, generally flat to Sachem Pond to the north
Surface:	Good; sandy in places
Traffic:	Heavy in Old Harbor, light elsewhere
Things to see:	Mohegan Bluffs, Southeast Light, Settler's Rock, North Light, Island Cemetery, Legion Park, New Harbor, Indian Cemetery, Old Harbor

Here is a ride that offers a rewarding minivacation for Long Islanders, providing at once a superb bicycling tour, travel on deep seas, and a visit to a displaced piece of New England, all in one day. Block Island sits 20 miles east of the eastern tip of Long Island and about 7 miles south of Rhode Island. It measures a mere 4 by 6 miles but provides spectacular seascape views and inviting rural charm on 20 miles or so of gently sloped roadways.

The ride route consists of a basic loop that explores the island's best scenic attractions on the western side facing Block Island Sound; on the southern and eastern parts facing the Atlantic, its main commercial and tourist center at Old Harbor; and an optional leg that runs to the island's sparsely populated north point. All of it can be enjoyed in the five hours or so between ferry trips, including time for lunch, but the north run can be dropped if you want to spend more time in Old Harbor.

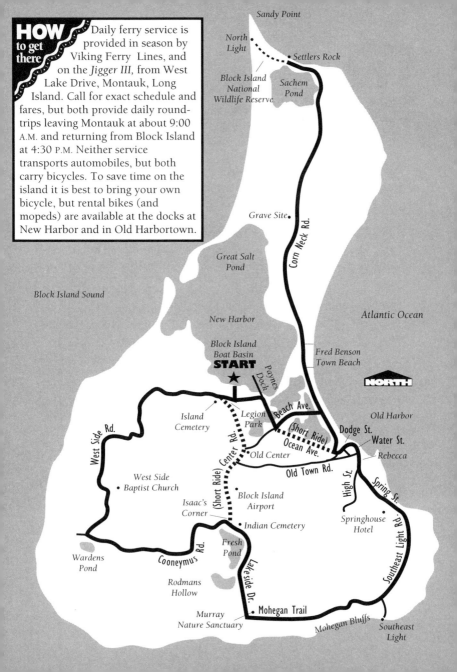

Sandy Point

North
Light
Settlers Rock

Block Island
National
Wildlife Reserve

Sachem
Pond

HOW to get there
Daily ferry service is provided in season by Viking Ferry Lines, and on the *Jigger III*, from West Lake Drive, Montauk, Long Island. Call for exact schedule and fares, but both provide daily round-trips leaving Montauk at about 9:00 A.M. and returning from Block Island at 4:30 P.M. Neither service transports automobiles, but both carry bicycles. To save time on the island it is best to bring your own bicycle, but rental bikes (and mopeds) are available at the docks at New Harbor and in Old Harbortown.

Grave Site

Corn Neck Rd.

Great Salt
Pond

Block Island Sound

New Harbor

Atlantic Ocean

Block Island
Boat Basin
START
★

Paynes
Dock

Fred Benson
Town Beach

NORTH

Island
Cemetery

Legion
Park

Beach Ave.

Old Harbor

West Side Rd.

Center Rd.

(Short Ride)

(Short Ride)
Ocean Ave.

Old Center

Dodge St.

Water St.

Rebecca

Old Town Rd.

West Side
Baptist Church

Isaac's
Corner

Block Island
Airport

High St.

Spring St.

Indian Cemetery

Springhouse
Hotel

Southeast Light Rd.

Fresh
Pond

Wardens
Pond

Cooneymus Rd.

Lakeside Dr.

Rodmans
Hollow

Murray
Nature Sanctuary

Mohegan Trail

Mohegan Bluffs

Southeast
Light

DIREC-TIONS at a glance

- Depart the ferry at the Block Island Boat Basin dock and proceed out to West Side Road.
- Right on West Side Road 2¾ miles to its end at Cooneymus Road.
- Left on Cooneymus Road for 1¼ miles to its end at Lakeside Drive–Center Road at Isaacs Corners. (The full ride continues right onto Lakeside Drive. A left turn onto Center Road takes you back to West Side Road at Veterans' Park, about a ¼ mile from the ride starting point.)
- Right on Lakeside Drive 1 mile to its end at Mohegan Trail.
- Left on Mohegan Trail, continuing onto Southeast Light Road and Spring Street, for 2 miles onto Water Street in Old Harbor town.
- The full ride proceeds on Water Street to Dodge Street and the run to Sachem Pond at the north end of the island. To skip the north run and return to the ride starting point, proceed left on Dodge Street one block and then across Old Town Road–Corn Neck Road onto Ocean Avenue. Continue on Ocean Avenue across Beach Avenue to the ferry dock on the right.
- For the full ride proceed on Dodge Street to the Old Town Road–Corn Neck Road intersection and then right onto Corn Neck Road.
- Continue on Corn Neck Road north for 4 miles to Sachem Pond, then return to Beach Avenue on the right.
- Right on Beach Avenue ¼ mile to Ocean Avenue.
- Right on Ocean Avenue ¼ mile to the ride starting point at the boat basin dock.

The ride begins from the pier in New Harbor on the Great Salt Pond. There is a great deal of activity on the pier and on the roads around the area at ferry time but it calms down quickly. Upon exiting the pier and turning right on West Side Road you immediately obtain a glimpse of the type of scenery you will see all along the route— broad cropped fields enclosed by rugged stone walls, providing the setting for handsome weathered homes and barns. Opposite is the water view. Great Salt Pond was once essentially landlocked, with only a trickle flowing from the sea through a narrow channel. Generations of Indians and later European colonists and island residents worked to keep it open. The task was completed by the federal government around 1900 when the harbor was opened for commerce. Today it is the site of the Block Island Boat Basin, with moorings for dozens of beautiful sailing craft and with Payne's Dock providing terminals for the Montauk Point ferries.

Continuing on West Side Road we come quickly to Legion Park and, just beyond, the Island Cemetery. Legion Park is a veterans' memorial containing stone tablets honoring veterans of World War II, Korea, and Vietnam in a tasteful, simple setting. The cemetery contains the gravesites of generations of Block Islanders, with some headstones dating from the 1700s. The inscriptions on many of the older headstones are obliterated from years of weathering on this windswept scenic site.

Bearing right at Legion Park we continue on West Side Road for about 3 miles. Expect some hills here, particularly farther on near Grace Cove Road. About halfway along we pass the West Side Baptist Church with a particularly good view west. The route proceeds left (east) at the end of West Side Road at Cooneymus Road.

At the foot of Cooneymus Road is Wardens Pond—an attractive pool typical of the multitude of ponds and lakes that dot Block Island—which provides sanctuary and habitat for migrating and local bird life. Cooneymus Road is about a 1-mile long, fairly flat stretch passing Rodman Hollow on the right. There is a fine view of the dense and varied vegetation of this deep cut, which is now protected from development by the Block Island Conservancy, an island-based environmental interest group. This leg of the ride ends at the intersection of Center Road and Lakeside Drive in an area called Isaac's Corner in honor of the island's last indigenous Indian.

Directly across the road, just south of the intersection, is the island's old Indian cemetery. This is a quiet grove containing simple fieldstone markers of the graves of the island's early residents. Opposite this and stretching south is Fresh Pond, a beautiful expanse of water surrounded by attractive homesites and fields. A stone marker at the head of the pond identifies it as the site at which, in 1661, the island's original European settlers established their first community.

At this point the full ride continues right (south) on Lakeside Drive, but by going left on Center Road, it also provides a short return to the ride starting point if you want to go back. The run back is a mile or so, mostly downhill, to West Side Road at Legion Park. Along the way you would pass the Block Island State Airport and, farther on, the intersection with Old Town Road. The intersection is known as the Old Center, it being the site of an earlier community consisting of stores, a school, workshops, the town hall, and other structures. All are gone now but remembered in a stone marker at the site.

Proceeding on Lakeside Drive we swoop down and around Fresh Pond for a mile or so, enjoying pleasant views all the way, and then climb a slight incline to the intersection with Mohegan Trail. At the intersection is a small benchmark noting this pleasant, quiet area as the Murray Nature Sanctuary.

From here on along Mohegan Trail and on into Old Harbor, a distance of about 2 miles, we encounter the most impressive sights and vistas the island has to offer, and, as a bonus, most of the run is downhill. Less than a mile along we come to Mohegan Bluffs, a 200-foot direct drop to the sea. A dirt path opening to a viewing platform, marked on the road as the Edward S. Payne Overlook, provides a spectacular view of the eroded bluffs and the crashing Atlantic surf that is slowly eating away at the island. For those with the energy, wooden stairs winding steeply down to the beach are provided for a look at the bluffs from below. Island lore has it that long ago an invading war party of mainland Mohegan Indians was captured by the island's indigenous Manissean tribe and as retribution for the attack was walked off these bluffs into the sea—a frightening prospect if true.

A few hundred yards farther along on Mohegan Trail is the famous Southeast Light, a well-known beacon for Block Island Sound mariners since 1875. It rises 204 feet above the sea and can be seen, it is said, from as far as 35 miles out. The building itself is an attractive

brick edifice, which until recently stood much closer to the bluff edge. The entire structure was moved inland 245 feet in 1993 to increase its distance from the constantly eroding bluff, insuring its stability for another 150 years or so.

Continuing on toward Old Harbor on Mohegan Trail and Southeast Road, we begin a long downhill run through a residential area of attractive homes, all of which capture the sea view, and then sweep on down toward the broad ocean and rock-strewn beaches in full view directly ahead. At the bottom of the hill on the left is the grand old Springhouse Hotel, the oldest hotel on the island, signaling our entry into the commercial center of the island. After a short uphill past the hotel we enter Old Harbor at Rebecca Circle from Spring Street and continue on Water Street to the heart of the village.

Old Harbor is a busy little port dependent on two large breakwaters whose embrace creates and protects the placid harbor and provides a safe haven for its complement of boats and ferries. The breakwaters were built in the 1880s, furnishing the island with an ocean port and ushering in a tourism and building boom that raised the hotels that line Water Street. Restaurants, boutiques, and shops of all kinds abound, and it's a great place for lunch and a rest. Keep in mind that Old Harbor is one of the few places on the island in which traffic can be heavy, especially during ferry arrivals or departures, so you might consider walking your bike when in town.

From Old Harbor the full ride goes north to the end of the island road at Sachem Pond. There and back, however, is an 8-mile run, and depending on how you feel and the amount of time remaining, you might wish to skip that portion of the ride and just laze around in Old Harbor. When ready to go, you can return to the ferry at New Harbor by continuing on Water Street to Dodge Street, continuing on Dodge across the four-way stop to Ocean, and continuing on Ocean across Beach Avenue to West Side Road and the ferry dock.

The full ride continues on Water Street to Dodge Street to the four-way stop at the intersection with Corn Neck Road. Turn right at the corner and proceed north on Corn Neck. This leg differs from the rest of the ride in that it is more beach oriented and goes through more open and less groomed areas. It is also narrower, with little shoulder room and faster traffic, so ride with care.

About a half mile north we come to Fred Benson Town Beach. It is a fully equipped facility on the ocean, providing an opportunity for a swim and a cold drink. Summer homes stand high on the dunes and hillocks opposite the beach, on the Great Salt Pond side of Corn Neck Road. Near here is a stone tablet marking the spot were Adrian Block, a Dutch explorer, came ashore in 1614, giving the island its name.

About halfway along, just past Mansion Beach Road, we pass a small enclosed cemetery containing the graves of members of the Sands and Thompson families, longtime residents of the island. About a half mile farther on, we begin a long descent to Sachem Pond at the end of Corn Neck Road. At the very end of the road is a stone marker identifying the spot as the site of the original founders landing in 1661. On that occasion a party of sixteen men with their families and animals came ashore and began the process of establishing homesteads and colonizing the island. The tablet lists their names, some of which are echoed in the street names and farms of the area.

To the north from Sachem Pond can be seen the North Light structure marking the northern extent of the island at Sandy Point. Although no longer operating, the light played a useful role for 150 years until its closure in 1972. There is no paved access to the lighthouse, but you can walk the half mile on the beach to the building for a close-up look. It is located in the middle of the area north of Sachem Pond that makes up the Block Island National Wildlife Refuge. From the lighthouse there is a unique and beautiful view of the beach, Sachem Pond, and the entire north quarter of the island.

We return to the ride starting point by going back on Corn Neck Road to Beach Road on the right, following it to Ocean Avenue and then right to West Side Road and the ride starting point at the dock.

It should be pointed out that the ride described is perfect for a one-day bicycling tour and covers just about every interesting feature of the island accessible by paved road. It by no means, however, exhausts all opportunities on the island. Given more time, one could explore off-road attractions accessible only on foot or in some cases by trail bike. These include numerous unpaved roads leading to the beaches and coves, the network of hiking trails in the Island Greenway threading from the middle of the island to its south shore, and the Clayhead Nature trail lying between Corn Neck Road and the ocean beach near Sachem Pond.

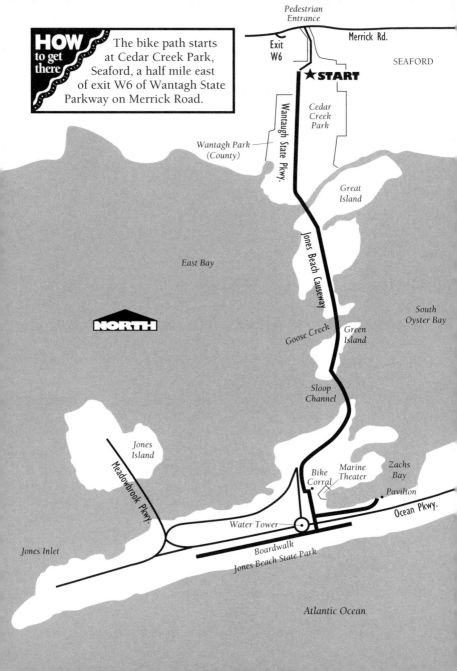

HOW to get there

The bike path starts at Cedar Creek Park, Seaford, a half mile east of exit W6 of Wantagh State Parkway on Merrick Road.

Pedestrian Entrance

Merrick Rd.

Exit W6

SEAFORD

★ START

Cedar Creek Park

Wantagh State Pkwy.

Wantagh Park (County)

Great Island

East Bay

NORTH

Jones Beach Causeway

Goose Creek

Green Island

South Oyster Bay

Sloop Channel

Jones Island

Meadowbrook Pkwy.

Bike Corral

Marine Theater

Zachs Bay

Pavilion

Ocean Pkwy.

Water Tower

Boardwalk

Jones Beach State Park

Jones Inlet

Atlantic Ocean

Jones Beach Bike Path

Miles of path: 5-mile path plus 2-mile boardwalk
Terrain: Flat
Surface: Paved

This is the premier bike path on Long Island. It runs south from Merrick Road for 5 miles on islands and over channels of the bays that separate the barrier beach from Long Island proper, and it provides the best bicycling experience available for this kind of terrain. Best of all, it terminates at Jones Beach, which itself is an unmatched oceanfront park with golf course, ball fields, skating rink, and other activities, plus numerous eateries. To best enjoy this ride, allow a full day for the complete circuit.

The path starts at Cedar Creek Park in Seaford and leads directly out onto a path paralleling Wantagh State Parkway. As it proceeds south on the Jones Beach Causeway, it crosses over three creeks on bridges from which you can see the boating, fishing, crabbing, and other bay activities that make this area so popular. Also visible is the landmark Jones Beach water tower.

The path ends at the Jones Beach Marine Theater. In the off-season, cyclists can continue through the theater parking lot to the beach, but in season, roughly from early April through September, bicycling is not allowed on the boardwalk, and bikes must be parked in a corral provided at the end of the path.

From here you can proceed to the beach directly across the parking lot, passing the Marine Theater on your left. Just past the theater is the Zachs Bay Bathing Beach, a calm-water alternative to the ocean beach. You can cycle around the southern portion of the bay on a well-paved path to a roofed pavilion from which you get a good view of the theater and Zachs Bay.

From Zachs Bay, continue to the east end of the boardwalk. The boardwalk runs for 2 miles past the attractions of Jones Beach.

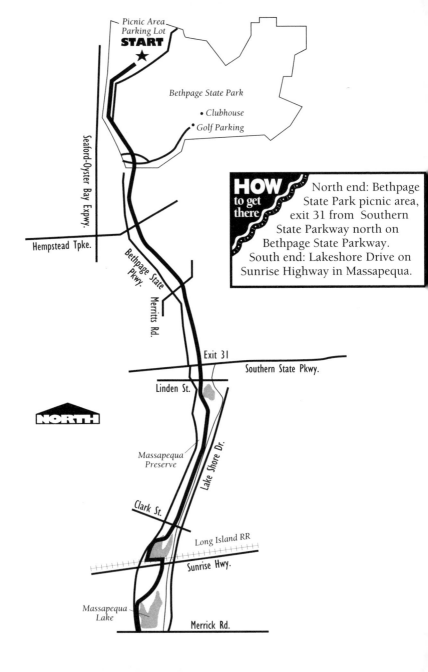

Picnic Area
Parking Lot
START

Bethpage State Park

• Clubhouse
• Golf Parking

Seaford-Oyster Bay Expwy.

Hempstead Tpke.

Bethpage State Pkwy.

Merritts Rd.

HOW to get there — North end: Bethpage State Park picnic area, exit 31 from Southern State Parkway north on Bethpage State Parkway. South end: Lakeshore Drive on Sunrise Highway in Massapequa.

Exit 31
Southern State Pkwy.

Linden St.

NORTH

Massapequa Preserve

Lake Shore Dr.

Clark St.

Long Island RR

Sunrise Hwy.

Massapequa Lake

Merrick Rd.

29 Bethpage State Park— Massapequa Preserve Bike Path

Miles of path: 8
Terrain: Generally flat; some hilly sections
Surface: All paved; sandy in places

This path runs from the middle of the Island in Bethpage to the south shore village of Massapequa, paralleling the southern section of the Nassau-Suffolk Greenbelt Trail. Despite the fact that it is in the heart of a densely populated area, it provides a quiet, bucolic environment that is rare in this part of the island.

The northern starting point of the path is the Bethpage State Park picnic area parking lot in the northwest corner of the park. The path runs south through the park over scenic and rather hilly terrain on an excellently paved path passing the Bethpage Park Polo Field. The path then skirts the western edge of the park, providing open views of the Blue and Yellow golf courses before exiting the park. For the next 2 miles or so the path runs along the Bethpage State Parkway where at points it comes quite close to the roadway as it swoops under overpasses. Also along this section are several road crossings requiring some care.

Just south of Southern State Parkway the path enters the Massapequa Preserve, where it follows the meanderings of slow-running streams through tranquil woods. This section of the path ends at Sunrise Highway in Massapequa, the southern starting point of the ride. The path continues on the south side of Sunrise Highway for ½ mile or so to Merrick Road through much the same type of quiet surroundings. The path can be picked up on the south side of the highway by crossing Sunrise at Lakeshore Drive and proceeding west a hundred yards or so to an unmarked opening opposite the path end on the north side of Sunrise. The view of Massapequa Lake at the Merrick Road end of the path is worth the extra effort.

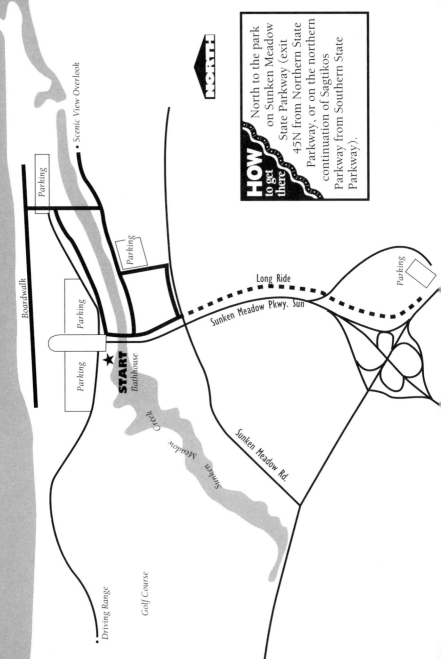

Long Island Sound

Boardwalk

Parking

Scenic View Overlook •

Parking

Parking

Parking

Parking

★
START
Bathhouse

Creek

Sunken Meadow

Golf Course

Driving Range •

Sunken Meadow Rd.

Sunken Meadow Pkwy. Sun

Long Ride

Parking

NORTH

HOW to get there

North to the park on Sunken Meadow State Parkway (exit 45N from Northern State Parkway, or on the northern continuation of Sagtikos Parkway from Southern State Parkway).

Sunken Meadow State Park

Miles of path: 2-mile path plus 1-mile boardwalk
Terrain: Flat in park area; uphill along parkway
Surface: Paved

This is a relatively short but challenging ride through a very scenic area that provides opportunities for a variety of bicycling experiences. It includes segments through wooded hills and a section along the beach on Long Island Sound.

The ride starts at the parking fields in front of the bathhouse in the main section of the park. It proceeds south over Sunken Meadow Creek and then east through wooded picnic areas. Toward its end in this direction the path begins to climb up toward a scenic overlook. At the very end is a paved platform that at one time probably gave an unobstructed view of the Sound. Trees and shrubs block the view from here today, but an even greater vista is available if you continue up the unpaved portion of the path to its highest point. This last segment is quite steep; that combined with the soft surface makes it necessary to walk instead of ride.

From this high vantage point you get a less obstructed view of the Sound and of the entire park area. On the horizon Connecticut is visible across Long Island Sound. In the foreground is the beach and Sunken Meadow Creek, which once made up most of the area. Most of this site was obtained by the state in 1928 and developed only gradually since then.

Returning from the overlook, we proceed over the creek on an attractive wooden piling-supported arch bridge to the bathhouse and boardwalk. The boardwalk runs for about 1 mile and is a pleasant stretch with open views of the Sound and its long, pebbly beaches. From here, for those who want a real workout, you can try the uphill climb on the bike path paralleling Sunken Meadow Parkway.

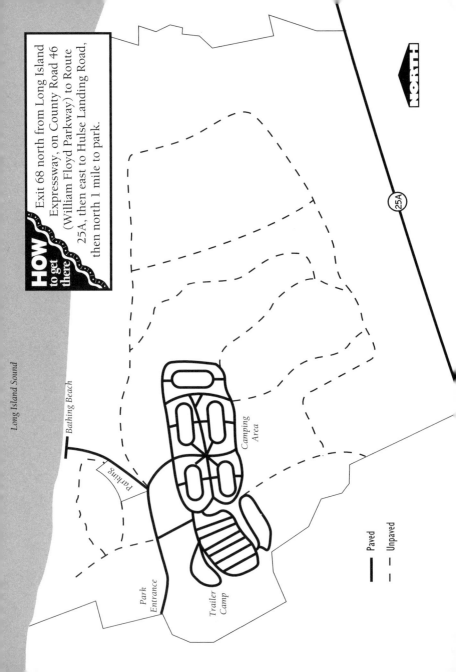

Long Island Sound

HOW to get there

Exit 68 north from Long Island Expressway, on County Road 46 (William Floyd Parkway) to Route 25A, then east to Hulse Landing Road, then north 1 mile to park.

NORTH

25A

Bathing Beach

Parking

Camping Area

Park Entrance

Trailer Camp

——— Paved
– – – Unpaved

Wildwood State Park

Miles of path: 12
Terrain: Hilly
Surface: 6 miles paved; 6 miles unpaved

Wildwood is a beautiful woodland park located on high bluffs over-looking Long Island Sound. Its main facilities are devoted to tent or trailer camping, and it features a fine bathing beach on the Sound. It is a relatively large park with an extensive array of roads and trails running through heavily wooded terrain. The roads winding around the camping and general recreation areas are paved, but in addition to these, bicycling is allowed on unpaved trails running through the un-developed eastern sections of the park. To ride these unpaved trails it is best to have a multispeed trail bike. These trails also are marked with warnings about the presence of deer ticks, sometime carriers of Lyme disease, advising that you keep well covered when on the trails.

Compared to most other parks on Long Island, the trails and roads here are somewhat hilly, especially around the outer ring of the tent campsites. The main path to the beach from the parking lot is so steep, in fact, that bicycles are not allowed on it. It's worth a walk down, however, to get to the beach and a short boardwalk from which you get a good view of the Connecticut hills 20 miles across Long Island Sound, the sand bluffs of the Long Island shoreline, and the stretch of pebble-strewn beach extending for miles in each direc-tion. At the head of the path is a bulletin board giving a short course on the species of fish in the sound and the allowable lengths of fish that can be taken from the water below.

The site was obtained by the state in 1925 from the Mitchell fam-ily of Babylon. The grounds were to be landscaped by the Olmsted brothers, designers of Central Park in New York City, but nothing re-mains of any groomed plantings. The park reflects its earlier, natural growth of large oak and pine.

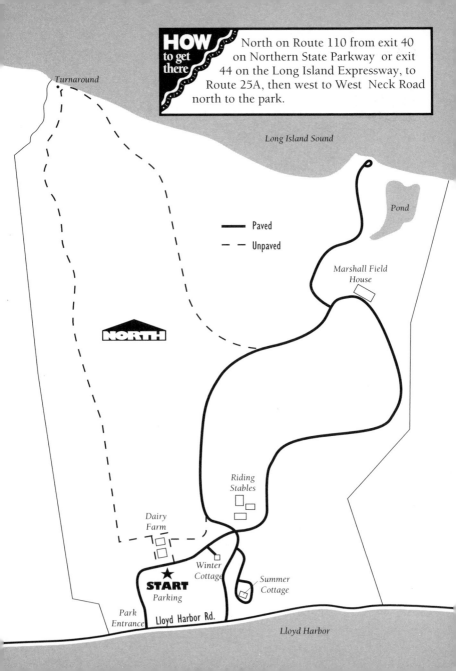

HOW to get there

North on Route 110 from exit 40 on Northern State Parkway or exit 44 on the Long Island Expressway, to Route 25A, then west to West Neck Road north to the park.

Turnaround

Long Island Sound

Pond

—— Paved
– – – Unpaved

Marshall Field House

NORTH

Riding Stables

Dairy Farm

★
START *Parking*

Winter Cottage

Summer Cottage

Park Entrance **Lloyd Harbor Rd.**

Lloyd Harbor

Caumsett State Park

Miles of path: 8
Terrain: Flat, with several hilly sections
Surface: 4 miles paved; 4 miles unpaved

Caumsett Park provides a variety of terrains for cycling. About half the paths are paved and half are somewhat challenging unpaved roads. The park also contains extensive hiking trails and bridle paths.

Caumsett is a relative newcomer to the roster of Long Island state parks, having been obtained by the state in 1961. It was the estate of Marshall Field III, grandson of the department-store magnate of the same name. The estate was developed in the 1920s as a self-contained country manor providing its own dairy products, vegetables, water and power supplies, and an extensive array of recreation facilities for the owner's guests.

The paved path starts from the parking lot and meanders for about 4 miles around the major structures of the park. It passes the winter and summer cottages, riding stables, and the Marshall Field main residence. Today the cottages house Board of Cooperative Educational Services (BOCES) educational programs and the main house is being leased by Queens College as the site for its Environmental Teaching and Research Center. Along this segment of the path one gets scenic views of the estate grounds and the great stands of woods.

The unpaved roads are quite challenging since they are steep and soft-surfaced in places. A multispeed all-terrain bike would be helpful here. The roads run through heavily treed woods and lead eventually to a turnaround overlooking Long Island Sound that provides great water views and a close-up look at the beach front.

On the return from the Sound back toward the ride starting point, the path runs past the estate dairy farm, an interesting complex of weathered buildings. Conveniently, there is a water fountain right here that is most welcome after the climb up from the Sound.

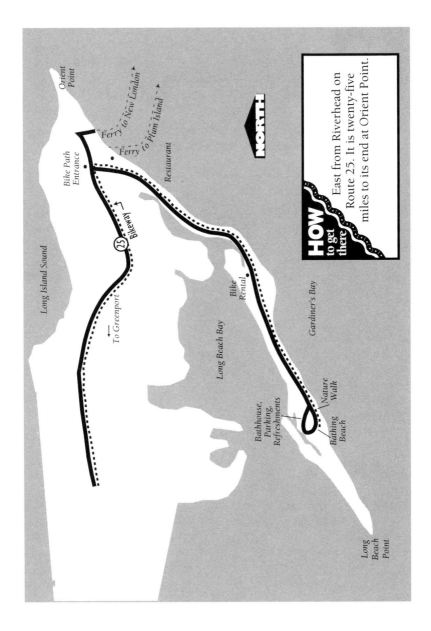

NORTH

HOW to get there
East from Riverhead on Route 25. It is twenty-five miles to its end at Orient Point.

Long Island Sound

Orient Point

Ferry to New London
Ferry to Plum Island

Bike Path Entrance

Restaurant

25 Bikeway

To Greenport

Bike Rental

Gardiner's Bay

Long Beach Bay

Bathhouse, Parking, Refreshments

Nature Walk

Bathing Beach

Long Beach Point

Orient Beach State Park

Miles of path: 3
Terrain: Flat
Surface: Paved

Orient Beach State Park lies at the tip of the North Fork and provides a run through a narrow neck of wooded land stretching far out into Gardiner's Bay. It is short but very pleasant ride on a well-paved path providing beautiful water views and the opportunity to observe water fowl (terns and ospreys) that are plentiful in the marshes and hillocks of the area. You can also get a view of the large ferries that run to New London, Connecticut, and the smaller boats that supply the government facility of Plum Island. The park features an excellent bathing beach and walking trail, and a small snack bar. It also offers bicycle rentals—the only state park on Long Island that does so. The pedestrian/cyclist entrance of the park connects to the bikeway shoulder of Route 25. The bikeway runs 9 miles or so the the village of Greenport.

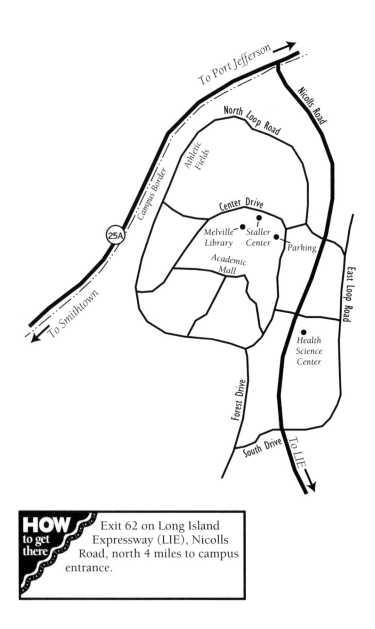

To Port Jefferson

Nicolls Road

North Loop Road

Campus Border

Athletic Fields

25A

Center Drive

Melville Library

Staller Center

Parking

Academic Mall

To Smithtown

East Loop Road

Health Science Center

Forest Drive

South Drive

To LIE

HOW to get there Exit 62 on Long Island Expressway (LIE), Nicolls Road, north 4 miles to campus entrance.

Stony Brook Campus

Miles of path: 4
Terrain: Mostly flat; some hilly sections
Surface: Paved

Stony Brook is an interesting place to visit and ride. It is a large campus with an excellent system of bike and pedestrian paths that offer many pleasant vistas and views. Like many State University of New York (SUNY) campuses, it is relatively new, dating only from the early 1960s. It expanded rapidly during the Rockefeller administration and reflects the immense investments made in those years in SUNY. This is most evident in the modern style and monumental (some would say overwhelming) scale of the architecture of some of the 121 campus buildings. The most interesting of these are the Health Sciences Center Towers, Academic Mall and surrounding buildings, and the steller Center for the Arts—Frank Melville Library complex.

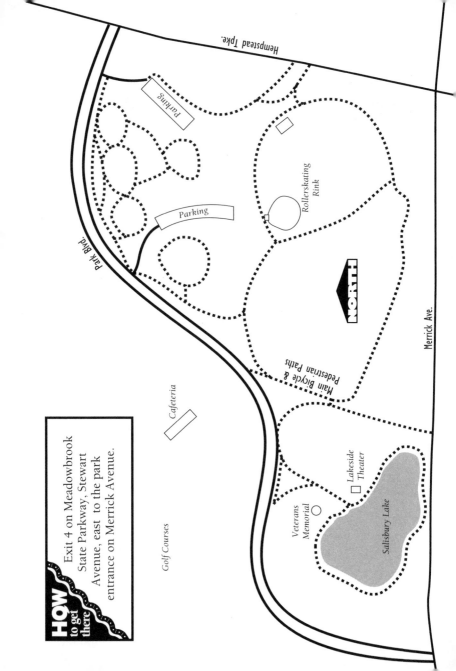

Hempstead Tpke.

Park Blvd.

Parking

Parking

Rollerskating
Rink

NORTH

Main Bicycle &
Pedestrian Paths

Merrick Ave.

Cafeteria

Golf Courses

Veterans
Memorial

Lakeside
Theater

Salisbury Lake

HOW to get there

Exit 4 on Meadowbrook
State Parkway, Stewart
Avenue, east to the park
entrance on Merrick Avenue.

Eisenhower Park

Miles of path: 5
Terrain: Flat
Surface: Paved

Eisenhower is a large Nassau County Park, most of which is devoted to golfing. The southwest section, however, contains a variety of recreation facilities, including a complex web of pedestrian and bike paths. These well-paved and well-maintained paths provide an interesting half day or so of bicycling. The paths explore every corner of the park, including Salisbury Lake, the Veterans Memorial, and Chapin Lakeside Theater in the north end and the innumerable athletic fields, picnic areas, and baseball diamonds, and outdoor roller rink in the south end. All in all, this is one of the best places in Nassau County for traffic-free bicycling.

Belmont Lake State Park

Miles of path: 3
Terrain: Flat
Surface: Paved, with some short sandy sections

The paths in this park meander around the beautiful one-time estate of August Belmont, who raised thoroughbred horses here. It was obtained by the state in 1926 and developed for use not only as the park we see today but as the site for the headquarters of the Long Island State Park Commission. The focus of the area is Belmont Lake, around which are ample bicycling and pedestrian paths and on which you can row the boats available for rental.

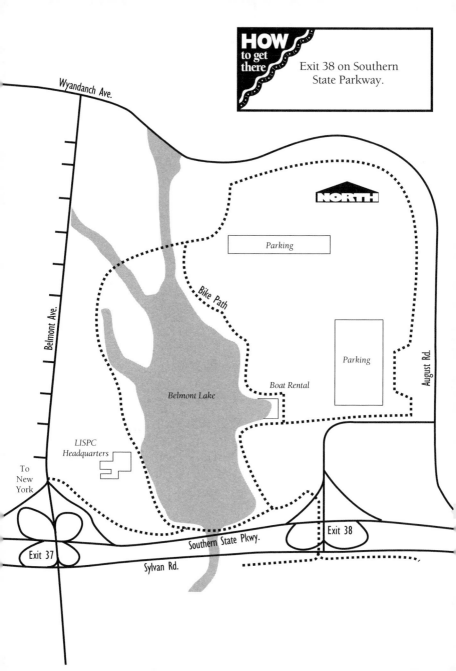

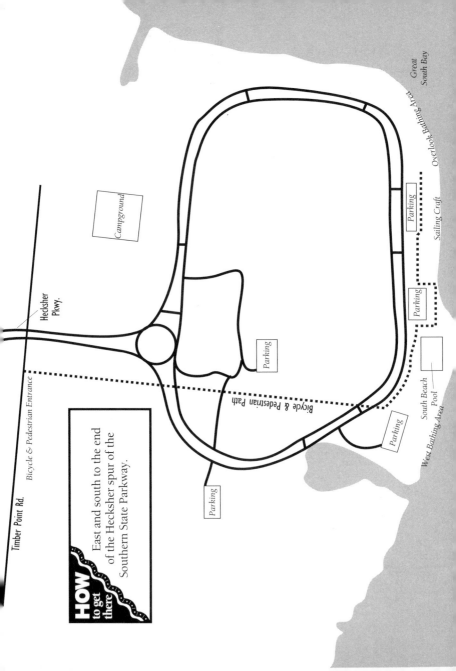

Timber Point Rd.

Bicycle & Pedestrian Entrance

Hecksher Pkwy.

Campground

Bicycle & Pedestrian Path

Parking

Parking

Parking

Parking

Parking

Parking

Sailing Craft

Overlook Bathing Area

Great South Bay

South Beach Pool

West Bathing Area

HOW to get there

East and south to the end of the Hecksher spur of the Southern State Parkway.

Hecksher State Park

Miles of path: 2
Terrain: Flat
Surface: Paved

This is an extremely easy and pleasant run through a copse of woods and open fields to broad beaches on Great South Bay. Swimming facilities are provided at Overlook and West beaches and in the Overlook pool. Interesting small sailing craft are launched from the beach adjacent to the pool and are fun to watch. At the east end of the park is the southern terminus of the Suffolk County Greenbelt hiking trail running north to Sunken Meadow Park on Long Island Sound.

Wantagh Park

Miles of path: 5
Terrain: Flat
Surface: Paved

Wantagh Park runs 2 miles south from Merrick Road to East Bay. It features an extensive network of walks and paths from which you can get fine views of the bay arms of Flat Creek and Johnson Creek, wetland marine life, and a variety of activities including fishing, baseball, waterskiing, and (my favorite) the often frustrating process of boat launching. After riding you can enjoy a quick swim in the large pool at the southern end of the park.

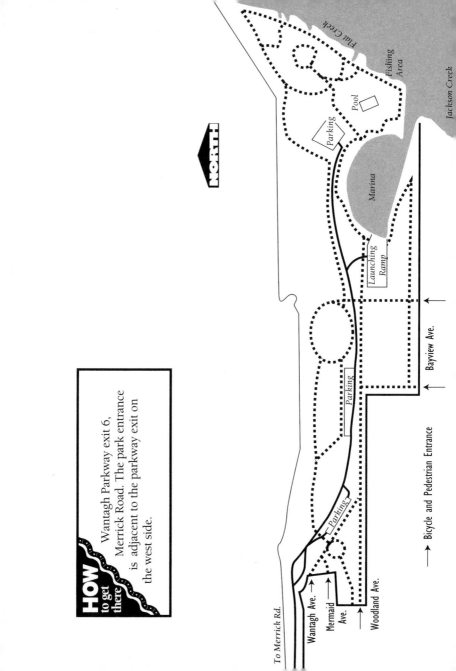

HOW to get there

Wantagh Parkway exit 6, Merrick Road. The park entrance is adjacent to the parkway exit on the west side.

NORTH

To Merrick Rd.

Flat Creek

Jackson Creek

Fishing Area

Pool

Parking

Marina

Launching Ramp

Parking

Parking

Bayview Ave.

Wantagh Ave.

Mermaid Ave.

Woodland Ave.

→ Bicycle and Pedestrian Entrance

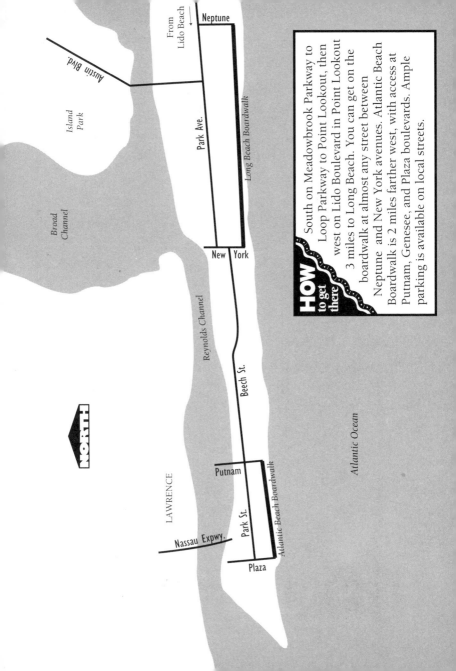

NORTH

From Lido Beach

Austin Blvd.

Neptune

Park Ave.

Long Beach Boardwalk

Island Park

Broad Channel

New York

Reynolds Channel

Beech St.

LAWRENCE

Putnam

Park St.

Nassau Expwy.

Plaza

Atlantic Beach Boardwalk

Atlantic Ocean

HOW to get there

South on Meadowbrook Parkway to Loop Parkway to Point Lookout, then west on Lido Boulevard in Point Lookout 3 miles to Long Beach. You can get on the boardwalk at almost any street between Neptune and New York avenues. Atlantic Beach Boardwalk is 2 miles farther west, with access at Putnam, Genesee, and Plaza boulevards. Ample parking is available on local streets.

39 Long Beach and Atlantic Beach Boardwalks

Miles of path: Long Beach—2 miles; Atlantic Beach—1 mile.

These boardwalks are great for a leisurely ride, especially during hot summer months. Both have clearly marked, broad bicycle lanes and direct access to the beach. The shore side is lined with hotels, condos, and cabanas. The Long Beach facility is larger and more active than Atlantic Beach and at several locations features snack bars and restaurants. Cycling is allowed year-round, and many riders take advantage of this freedom using the path and enjoying the ocean vista even in winter.

Valley Stream State Park

Miles of path: 4
Terrain: Flat
Surface: Paved

Valley Stream Park is one of the oldest of Long Island's state parks. Close to the New York City border in a densely populated area, it quickly became and remains an extremely popular facility. It is smaller than most of the parks of the system but contains 2 miles or so of paths through heavily treed terrain. As a bonus, it ties directly into Hendrickson Park to the south, which extends the path for 2 additional miles around Valley Stream Pond.

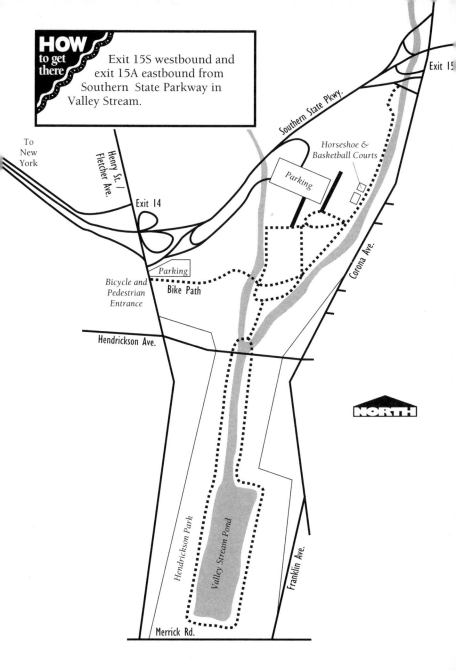

HOW to get there

Exit 15S westbound and exit 15A eastbound from Southern State Parkway in Valley Stream.

To New York

Henry St. / Fletcher Ave.

Exit 14

Southern State Pkwy.

Exit 15

Horseshoe & Basketball Courts

Parking

Corona Ave.

Parking

Bicycle and Pedestrian Entrance

Bike Path

Hendrickson Ave.

NORTH

Hendrickson Park

Valley Stream Pond

Franklin Ave.

Merrick Rd.

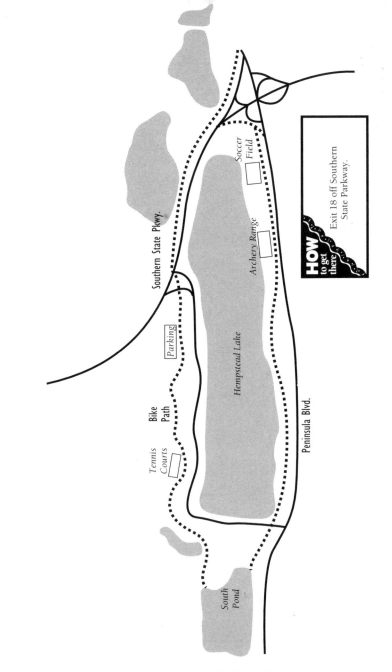

Southern State Pkwy.

Soccer Field

Archery Range

Parking

Bike Path

Tennis Courts

Hempstead Lake

Peninsula Blvd.

South Pond

HOW to get there
Exit 18 off Southern State Parkway.

Hempstead Lake State Park

Miles of path: 4
Terrain: Flat
Surface: Paved

This park was developed around Hempstead Lake and several smaller ponds and provides facilities for picnicking, soccer, baseball, tennis, and archery. The bike path encircles Hempstead Lake, paralleling an exercise course and equestrian path. On the east side of the lake the path runs for a pleasant mile through a dense stand of woods. At the north end, however, the path closely parallels the northern side of Southern State Parkway. Getting to the north side of the parkway requires crossing heavily trafficked exit ramps. For the leisurely rider it would be best to avoid these crossings and stay in the southern part of the park.

Bikeways

New York State, in conjunction with local planning agencies, has been developing a plan for the construction of a network of bicycling paths that would provide links for nonmotorized traffic within and between important recreational and commercial areas in the state. The program consists mainly of adding or widening the shoulders of existing roads and constructing new traffic-free paths for bicyclists. Most of the work is being paid for by the federal government.

The Long Island portion of the plan consists of hundreds of miles of paths and shoulders that would provide a multitude of opportunities for enjoyable bicycling tours. The project, however, is only in the planning stage, with considerable work yet to be done in obtaining the authorizations and funding required to actually implement the plans. Most of the park paths described in this book have been made part of the bikeway system, and several roads in Suffolk County have been modified and designated as bikeways. At this time the best of the road bikeways for the casual cyclist are shown below. The list will expand to twenty-five or thirty such routes as the program evolves.

- •Greenport to Orient Point: a 9-mile run on wide shoulders along Route 25 on the North Fork. This is a scenic stretch, connecting Orient Beach State Park to the village of Greenport, which provides a mix water and farm views with many opportunities for rest and refreshments.

- • Sag Harbor to North Haven: a 4-mile route on the shoulder of Route 114 that runs from historic whaling village of Sag Harbor to the Shelter Island Ferry slip in North Haven. The ride has some hills, but the views of the village and the surrounding waters are interesting.

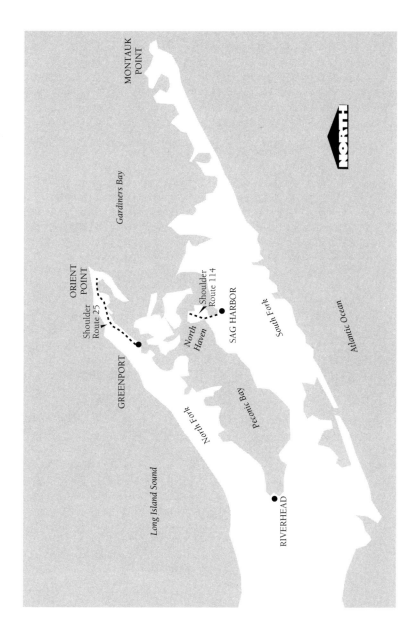